Captives!

Captives!

The Narratives of seven women
taken prisoner by the Plains Indians
of the American West

Cynthia Ann Parker
Mrs Jannette E. De Camp Sweet
Mary Schwandt
Mrs. Caroline Harris
Misses Frances and Almira Hall
Nancy McClure

LEONAUR

Captives!
The Narratives of seven women taken prisoner
by the Plains Indians of the American West
Cynthia Ann Parker
Mrs Jannette E. De Camp Sweet
Mary Schwandt
Mrs. Caroline Harris
Misses Frances and Almira Hall
Nancy McClure

First published under the titles
Cynthia Ann Parker, the Story of Her Capture
Mrs. J. E. De Camp Sweet's Narrative
of Her Captivity in the Sioux Outbreak of 1862,
The Story of Mary Schwandt,
History of the Captivity and Providential Release Therefrom
of Mrs. Caroline Harris,
(As part of) *Narrative of the Capture and Providential Escape*
of Misses Frances and Almira Hall
and
The Story of Nancy McClure

FIRST EDITION

Leonaur is an imprint of Oakpast Ltd

Copyright in this form © 2010 Oakpast Ltd

ISBN: 978-0-85706-206-2 (hardcover)
ISBN: 978-0-85706-205-5 (softcover)

http://www.leonaur.com

Publisher's Notes

In the interests of authenticity, the spellings, grammar and place names used have been retained from the original editions.

The opinions of the authors represent a view of events in which she was a participant related from her own perspective, as such the text is relevant as an historical document.

The views expressed in this book are not necessarily those of the publisher.

Contents

Cynthia Ann Parker

Preface

In the month of June, 1884, there appeared in the columns of the Forth Worth *Gazette* an advertisement signed by the Comanche chief, Quanah Parker, and dated from the reservation near Fort Sill, in the Indian Territory, enquiring for a photograph of his late mother, Cynthia Ann Parker, which served to revive interest in a tragedy which has always been enveloped in a greater degree of mournful romance and pathos than any of the soul-stirring episodes of our pioneer life, so fruitful of incidents of an adventurous nature.

From the valued narratives kindly furnished us by Victor M. Ross, Major John Henry Brown and Gen. L. S. Ross, supplemented by the Jas. W. Parker book and copious notes from Hon. Ben. F. Parker, together with most of the numerous partial accounts of the fall of Parker's Fort and subsequent relative events, published during the past fifty years; and after a careful investigation and study of the whole, we have laboriously and with much painstaking, sifted out and evolved the foregoing narrative of plain, unvarnished facts, which form a part of the romantic history of Texas.

In the preparation of our little volume the thanks of the youthful author are due to Gen. L. S. Ross, of Waco; Major John Henry Brown of Dallas; Gen. Walter P. Lane of Marshall; Col. John S. Ford of San Antonio; Rev. Homer S. Thrall—the eminent historian of Texas; Mr. A. F. Corning of Waco; Capt. Lee Hall, Indian Agent, I. T., and Mrs. C. A. Westbrook of Lorena, for valuable assistance rendered.

To Victor M. Ross of Laredo, Texas, the author has been placed under many and lasting obligations for valuable data so generously placed at his disposal, and that too at considerable sacrifice to the donor.

From this source we have obtained much of the matter for our

CYNTHIA ANN PARKER

narrative.

In submitting our little work—the first efforts of the youthful author—we assure the reader that while there are, doubtless, many defects and imperfections, he is not reading fiction, but facts which form only a part of the tragic and romantic history of the Lone Star State.

James T. Deshields,

Belton, Texas, May 19, 1886.

Chapter 1
The Parker Port Massacre, etc.

Contemporary with, and among the earliest of the daring and hardy pioneers that penetrated the eastern portion of the Mexican province of Texas, were the "Parker family," who immigrated from Cole county, Illinois, in the fall of the year 1833, settling on the west side of the Navasota creek, near the site of the present town of Groesbeck, in Limestone county, one or two of the family coming a little earlier and some a little later.

The elder John Parker was a native of Virginia, resided for a time in Elbert county, Georgia, but chiefly reared his family in Bedford county, Tennessee, whence in 1818 he removed to Illinois.

The family, with perhaps one or two exceptions, belonged to one branch of the primitive Baptist church, commonly designated as "two seed," or "hard shell" Baptists.

In the spring of 1834 the colonist erected Parker's Fort,[1] a kind of wooden barricade, or wall around their cabins, which served as a means of better protecting themselves against the numerous predatory

---

1. The reader will understand by this term, not only a place of defence, but the residence of a small number of families belonging to the same neighbourhood. As the Indian mode of warfare was an indiscriminate slaughter of all ages, and both sexes, it was as requisite to provide for the safety of the women and children as for that of the men. Dodridge's faithful pen picture of early pioneer forts, will perhaps give the reader a glimpse of old Fort Parker in the dark and bloody period of its existence. He says:

"The fort consisted of cabins, blockhouses, and stockades. A range of cabins commonly formed on one side at least of the fort. Divisions, or portions of logs, separated the cabins from each other. The walls on the outside were ten or twelve feet high, the slope of the roof being turned wholly inward. A very few of these cabins had puncheon floors, the greater part were earthen. The blockhouses were built at the angles of the fort. They projected about two feet beyond the outer walls of the cabins and stockades. Their upper stories were about eighteen inches every way larger in dimension than the under one, leaving an opening at the commencement of the second to prevent the enemy from (continued next page.)

bands of Indians into that, then, sparsely settled section.

As early as 1829 the "Prairie Indians" had declared war against the settlers, and were now actively hostile, constantly committing depredations in different localities.

Parker's colony at this time consisted of only some eight or nine families, *viz*: Elder John Parker, patriarch of the family, and his wife; his son James W. Parker, wife, four single children and his daughter, Mrs. Rachel Plummer, her husband, L. M. T. Plummer, and infant son, fifteen months old; Mrs. Sarah Nixon, another daughter, and her husband L. D. Nixon; Silas M. Parker (another son of Elder John), his wife and four children Benjamin F. Parker, an unmarried son of the Elder [2]; Mrs. Nixon, sr., mother of Mrs. James W. Parker; Mrs. Elizabeth Kellogg, daughter of Mrs. Nixon; Mrs. —— Duty; Samuel M. Frost, wife and two children; G. E. Dwight, wife and two children in all thirty-four persons.

Besides those above mentioned, old man—Lunn, David Faulkenberry and his son Evan, Silas Bates, and Abram Anglin, a boy, had erected cabins a mile or two distant from the fort, where they resided.

These families were truly the advance guard of civilization of that part of our frontier. Fort Houston, in Anderson county, being the nearest protection, except their own trusty rifles.

Here the struggling colonist remained, engaged in the avocations

---

making a lodgement under their walls. In some forts, instead of blockhouses the angles of the fort were furnished with bastions. A large folding gate, made of thick slabs, nearest the spring, closed the fort. The stockades, bastions, cabins, and blockhouse walls, were furnished with port-holes at proper heights and distances. The whole of the outside was completely bullet-proof.

It may be truly said that "necessity is the mother of invention"; for the whole of this work was made without the aid of a single nail or spike of iron; and for this reason such things were not to be had. In some places, less exposed, a single blockhouse, with a cabin or two, constituted the whole fort. Such places of refuge may appear very trifling to those who have been in the habit of seeing the formidable military garrisons of Europe and America, but they answered the purpose, as the Indians had no artillery. They seldom attacked, and scarcely ever took one of them."

2. Elder Daniel Parker, a man of strong mental powers, a son of Elder John, does not figure in these events. He signed the Declaration of Independence in 1836, and preached to his people till his death in Anderson county in 1845. Ex-Representative Ben. F. Parker, is his son and successor in preaching at the same place. Isaac Parker, above mentioned, another son, long represented Houston and Anderson counties in Senate and House, and in 1855 represented Tarrant county. He died in Parker county, not long since, not far from 88 years of age. Isaac D. Parker of Tarrant is his son.

of a rural life, tilling the soil, hunting buffalo, bear, deer, turkeys and smaller game, which served abundantly to supply their larder at all times with fresh meat, in the enjoyment of a life of Arcadian simplicity, virtue and contentment, until the latter part of the year 1835, when the Indians and Mexicans forced the little band of compatriots to abandon their homes, and flee with many others before the invading army from Mexico.

On arriving at the Trinity River they were compelled to halt in consequence of an overflow. Before they could cross the swollen stream the sudden and unexpected news reached them that Santa Anna and his vandal hordes had been confronted and defeated at San Jacinto, that sanguinary engagement which gave birth to the new sovereignty of Texas, and that *Texas was free from Mexican tyranny.*

On receipt of this news the fleeing settlers were overjoyed, and at once returned to their abandoned homes.

The Parker colony now retraced their steps, first going to Fort Houston, where they remained a few days in order to procure supplies, after which they made their way back to Fort Parker to look after their stock and to prepare for a crop.

These hardy sons of toil spent their nights in the fort, repairing to their farms early each morning.

On the night of May 18, 1836, all slept at the fort, James W. Parker, Nixon and Plummer repairing to their field a mile distant on the Navasota, early next morning, little thinking of the great calamity that was soon to befall them.

About 9 o'clock a. m. the fort was visited by several hundred[3] Comanche and Kiowa Indians. On approaching to within about three hundred yards of the fort the Indians halted in the prairie, presenting a white flag; at the same time making signs of friendship.

At this time there were only six men in the fort, three having gone out to work in the field as above stated. Of the six men remaining, only five were able to bear arms, *viz*: Elder John Parker, Benjamin and Silas Parker, Samuel and Robert Frost. There were ten women and fifteen children.

The Indians, artfully feigning the treacherous semblance of friendship, pretended that they were looking for a suitable camping place, and enquired as to the exact locality of a water-hole in the vicinity, at

---

3. Different accounts have variously estimated the number of Indians at from 300 to 700. One account says 300, another 500, and still another 700. There were perhaps about 500 warriors.

11

the same time asking for a beef to appease their hungry a want always felt by an Indian, when the promise of fresh meat loomed up in the distant perspective; and he would make such pleas with all the servile sicophancy of a slave, like the Italian who embraces his victim ere plunging the poniard into his heart.

Not daring to resent so formidable a body of savages, or refuse to comply with their requests, Mr. Benjamin F. Parker went out to them, had a talk and returned, expressing the opinion that the Indians were hostile and intended to fight, but added that he would go back and try to avert it. His brother Silas remonstrated, but he persisted in going, and was immediately surrounded and killed, whereupon the whole force their savage instincts aroused by the sight of blood—charged upon the works, uttering the most terrific and unearthly yells that ever greeted the ears of mortals. Cries and confusion reigned. The sickening and bloody tragedy was soon enacted.

Brave Silas M. Parker fell on the outside of the fort, while he was gallantly fighting to save Mrs. Plummer. Mrs. Plummer made a most manful resistance, but was soon overpowered, knocked down with a hoe and made captive. Samuel M. Frost and his son Robert met their fate while heroically defending the women and children inside the stockade. Old Granny Parker was outraged, stabbed and left for dead. Elder John Parker, wife and Mrs. Kellogg attempted to make their escape, and in the effort had gone about three-fourths of a mile, when they were overtaken and driven back near to the fort where the old gentleman was stripped, murdered, scalped and horribly mutilated. Mrs. Parker was stripped, speared and left for dead, but by feigning death escaped, as will be seen further on. Mrs. Kellogg was spared as a captive.

The result summed up, was as follows:

Killed—Elder John Parker, aged seventy-nine; Silas M. and Benjamin F. Parker; Samuel M. and his son Robert Frost.

Wounded dangerously—Mrs. John Parker; Old Granny Parker and Mrs. —— Duty.

Captured—Mrs. Rachel Plummer, (daughter of James W. Parker), and her son James Pratt Plummer, two years of age; Mrs. Elizabeth Kellogg; Cynthia Ann Parker, nine years old, and her little brother John Parker, aged six years, children of Silas M. Parker. The remainder of the inmates making their escape, as we shall narrate.

When the attack on the fort first commenced, Mrs. Sarah Nixon made her escape and hastened to the field to advise her father, husband and Plummer. On her arrival, Plummer hurried on horseback to inform the Faulkenberrys, Limn, Bates and Anglin. Parker and Nixon started to the fort, but the former met his family on the way, and carried them some five miles down the Navasota, secreting them in the bottom. Nixon, though unarmed, continued on towards the fort, and met Mrs. Lucy, wife of the dead Silas Parker, with her four children, just as they were intercepted by a small party of mounted and foot Indians. They compelled the mother to lift behind two mounted warriors her daughter Cynthia Ann, and her little son John. The foot Indians now took Mrs. Parker, her two youngest children and Nixon back to the fort.

Just as the Indians were about to kill Nixon, David Faulkenberry appeared with his rifle, and caused them to fall back. Nixon, after his narrow escape from death, seemed very much excited, and immediately left in search of his wife, soon falling in with Dwight, with his own and Frost's family. Dwight and party soon overtook J. W. Parker and went with him to the hiding place in the bottom.

Faulkenberry, thus left with Mrs. Parker and her two children, bade her to follow him. With the infant in her arms and leading the other child she obeyed. Seeing them leave the fort, the Indians made several feints, but were held in check by the brave man's rifle. Several mounted warriors, armed with bows and arrows strung and drawn, and with terrific yells would charge them, but as Faulkenberry would present his gun they would halt, throw up their shields, right about, wheel and retire to a safe distance. This continued for some distance, until they had passed through a prairie of some forty or fifty acres.

Just as they were entering the woods, the Indians made a desperate charge, when one warrior, more daring than the others, dashed up so near that Mrs. Parker's faithful dog seized his horse by the nose, whereupon both horse and rider somersaulted, alighting on their backs in a ravine. Just at this moment Silas Bates, Abram Anglin and Evan Faulkenberry, armed, and Plummer unarmed, came up, causing the Indians to retire, after which the party made their way unmolested.

As they were passing through the field where the three men had been at work in the morning, Plummer, as if aroused from a dream, demanded to know what had become of his wife and child. Armed only with a butcher knife, he left the party, in search of his loved ones, and was seen no more for six days.

The Faulkenberrys, Lunn, with Mrs. Parker and children, secreted themselves in a small creek bottom, some distance from the first party, each unconscious of the other's whereabouts.

At twilight Abraham Anglin and Evan Faulkenberry started back to the fort to succour the wounded and those who might have escaped. On their way, and just as they were passing Faulkenberry's cabin, Anglin saw his first and only ghost. He says:

> It was dressed in white with long, white hair streaming down its back. I admit that I was worse scared at this moment than when the Indians were yelling and charging us. Seeing me hesitate, my ghost now beckoned me to come on. Approaching the object it proved to be old Granny Parker, whom the Indians had wounded and stripped, with the exception of her underwear. She had made her way to the house from the fort by crawling the entire distance. I took some bed clothing, and carrying her some distance from the house, made her a bed, covered her up and left her until we should return from the fort.
>
> On arriving at the fort we could not see a single individual alive or hear a human sound. But the dogs were barking, the cattle lowing, the horses neighing and the hogs squealing, making a hideous and strange medley of sounds. Mrs. Parker had told me where she had left some silver, $106.50. This I found under a hickory bush by moonlight. Finding no one at the fort we returned to where I had hid Granny Parker. On taking her up behind me, we made our way back to our hiding place in the bottom, where we found Nixon, whom we had not seen since his cowardly flight at the time he was rescued by Faulkenberry from the Indians. [4]

On the next morning, Bates, Anglin and E. Faulkenberry went back to the fort to get provisions and horses and to look after the dead. On reaching the fort they found five or six horses, a few saddles and some meal, bacon and honey. Fearing an attack from the red devils who might still be lurking around, they left without burying the dead. Returning to their comrades in the bottom, they all concealed themselves until the next night, when they started through the woods to

---

4. In the book published by James W. Parker on pages ten and eleven, he states that Nixon liberated Mrs. Parker from the Indians and rescued old Granny Parker. Mr. Anglin, in his account contradicts, or rather corrects this statement. He says: "I positively assert that this is a mistake and I am willing to be qualified to the statement I here make and can prove the same by Silas H. Bates, now living near Graesbeck."

Fort Houston, which place they reached without material suffering.

Fort Houston, an asylum on this as on many other occasions, stood on what has been for many years the farm of a wise statesman, a chivalrous soldier and a true patriot—John H. Reagan—two miles west of Palestine.

After wandering around and travelling for six days and nights, during which time they suffered much from hunger and thirst, with their clothing torn into shreds, their bodies lacerated with briars and thorns, the women and children with unshod and bleeding feet, the party of James W. Parker ———— men, and ————[5] women and children reached Tinnin's, at the old San Antonio and Nacogdoches crossing of the Navasota. Being informed of their approach, Messrs. Carter and Courtney, with five horses, met them some miles away, and thus enabled the women and children to ride. The few people around, though but returned to their deserted homes after the victory of San Jacinto, shared all they had of food and clothing with them.

Plummer, after six days of wanderings alone in the wilderness, arrived at the fort the same day.

In due time the members of the party located temporarily as best suited the respective families, most of them returning to Fort Parker soon afterwards.

A burial party of twelve men from Fort Houston went up and buried the dead. Their remains now repose near the site of old Fort Parker. Peace to their memories. Unadorned are their graves; not even a slab of marble or a memento of any kind has been erected to tell the traveller where rests the remains of this brave little band of pioneer heroes who wrestled with the savage for the mastery of this proud domain.

After the massacre the savages retired with their booty to their own wild haunts amid the hills and valleys of the beautiful Canadian and Pease Rivers.

CHAPTER 2

THE CAPTIVES CYNTHIA ANN AND JOHN PARKER

Of the captives we will briefly trace their subsequent checkered career.

After leaving the fort the two tribes, the Comanches and Kiowas, remained and travelled together until midnight. They then halt-

---

5. We are unable to ascertain the exact number. Different accounts variously estimate the number from 10 to 20.

ed on an open prairie, staked out their horses, placed their pickets, and pitched their camp. Bringing all their prisoners together for the first time, they tied their hands behind them with rawhide thongs so tightly as to cut the flesh, tied their feet close together, and threw them upon their faces. Then the braves, gathering around with their yet bloody, dripping scalps, commenced their usual war dance. They danced, screamed, yelled, stamping upon their prisoners, beating them with bows until their own blood came near strangling them. The remainder of the night these frail women suffered and had to listen to the cries and groans of their tender little children.

Mrs. Elizabeth Kellogg, soon fell into the hands of the Keechis, from whom, six months after her capture, she was purchased by a party of Delawares, who carried her into Nacogdoches and delivered her to Gen. Houston, who paid them $150.00, the amount they had paid and all they asked.

On the way thence to Fort Houston, escorted by James W. Parker and others, a hostile Indian was slightly wounded and temporarily disabled by a Mr. Smith. Mrs. Kellogg instantly recognized him as the savage who had scalped the patriarch, Elder John Parker, whereupon, without judge, jury or court-martial, or even dallying with "Judge Lynch," he was involuntarily hastened to the "happy hunting grounds" of his fathers.

Mrs. Rachel Plummer remained a captive about eighteen months. Soon after her capture she was delivered of a child. The crying of her infant annoyed her captors, and the mother was forced to yield up her offspring to the merciless fiends,—in whose veins the milk of human sympathy had never flowed, to be murdered before her eyes with all the demoniacal demonstrations of brutality intact in those savages. The innocent little babe but six weeks old was torn madly from the mother's bosom by six giant Indians, one of them clutched the little prattling innocent by the throat, and like a hungry beast with defenceless prey, he held it out in his iron grasp until all evidence of life seemed extinct. Mrs. Plummer's feeble efforts to save her child were utterly fruitless. They tossed it high in the air and repeatedly let it fall on rocks and frozen earth.

Supposing the child dead they returned it to its mother, but discovering traces of lingering life, they again, by force, tore it angrily from her, tied plaited ropes around its neck and threw its unprotected body into hedges of prickly pear. They would repeatedly pull it through these lacerating rushes with demonic yells. Finally, they tied the rope attached to its neck to the pommel of a saddle and rode triumphantly around a circuit until it was not only dead but literally torn to shreds. All that remained of that once beautiful babe was then tossed into the lap of its poor, distracted mother. With an old knife the weeping mother was allowed to dig a grave and bury her babe.

After this she was given as a servant to a very cruel old squaw, who treated her in a most brutal manner. Her son had been carried off by another party to the far West and she supposed her husband and father had been killed at the massacre. Her infant was dead, and death to her would have been a sweet relief. Life was a burden, and driven almost to desperation, she resolved no longer to submit to the intolerant old squaw. One day when the two were some distance from, although still in sight of the camp, her mistress attempted to beat her with a club. Determined not to submit to this, she wrenched the club from the hands of the squaw and knocked her down.

The Indians, who had witnessed the whole proceedings from their camp, now came running up, shouting at the top of their voices. She fully expected to be killed, but they patted her on the shoulder, crying, "*Bueno! bueno!!*' (Good! good!!)) or well done! She now fared much better and soon became a great favourite and was known as the "Fighting Squaw." She was eventually ransomed through the agency of some Mexican Santa Fe traders, by a noble-hearted, American merchant of that place, Mr. William Donahue. She was purchased in the Rocky Mountains so far north of Santa Fe that seventeen days were consumed in reaching that place. She was at once made a member of her benefactor's family, where she received the kindest of care and attention. Ere long she accompanied Mr. and Mrs. Donahue on a visit to Independence, Missouri, where she had the pleasure of meeting and embracing her brother-in-law, L. D. Nixon, and by him was escorted back to her people in Texas.[1]

On the 19th of February, 1838, she reached her father's house, exactly twenty-one months from her capture. She had never seen her

---

1. During her stay with the Indians, Mrs. Plummer had many thrilling adventures, which she often related after her reclamation. In narrating her reminiscences, she said that in one of her rambles, after she had been with the Indians some time, she discovered a cave in the mountains, and in company with the old squaw that guarded her, she explored it and found a large diamond, but her mistress immediately demanded it, and she was forced to give it up. She said also here in these mountains she saw a bush which had thorns on it resembling fish-hooks which the Indians used to catch fish with, and she herself has often caught trout with them in the little mountain streams.

little son, James Pratt, since soon after their capture, and knew nothing of his fate. She wrote, or dictated a thrilling and graphic history of her capture and the horrors of her captivity of the tortures and hardships she endured, and all the incidents of her life with her captors, with observations among the savages. [2] In this book she tells the last she saw of Cynthia Ann and John Parker. She died on the 19th of February, 1839, just one year after reaching home. As a remarkable coincidence it may be stated that she was born on the 19th, married on the 19th, captured on the 19th, released on the 19th, reached Independence on the 19th, arrived at home on the 19th, and died on the 19th of the month.

Her son, James Pratt Plummer, after six long and weary years of captivity and suffering, during which time he had lived among many different tribes and travelled several thousand miles, was ransomed and taken to Fort Gibson late in 1842, and reached home in February, 1843, in charge of his grandfather. He became a respected citizen of Anderson county. Both he and his father are now dead.

This still left in captivity Cynthia and John Parker, who, as subsequently learned,. were held by separate bands. The brother and sister thus separated, gradually forgot the language, manners and customs of their own people, and became thorough Comanches as the long years stole slowly away. How long the camera of their young brains retained impressions of the old home within the fort, and the loved faces of their pale-faced kindred, no one knows; though it would appear that the fearful massacre should have stamped an impress indelible while life continued. But the young mind, as the twig, is inclined by present circumstances, and often forced in a way wholly foreign to its native and original bent.

John grew up with the little semi-nude Comanche boys of his own age, and played at "hunter" and "warrior" with pop-guns made of the elder stem, or bows and arrows, and often flushed the *chaparral* for hare and grouse, or entrapped the finny denizens of the mountain brooks with the many peculiar and ingenious devices of the wild man for securing for his repast the toothsome trout which abounds so

---

2.—This valuable and interesting little book is now rare, scarce and out of print. The full title of the volume is:

Narration of the Perilous Adventures, miraculous escapes and sufferings of Rev. Jas. W. Parker, during a frontier residence in Texas of fifteen years. With an impartial geographical description of the climate, soil, timber, water, etc., of Texas. To which is appended the narrative of the capture and subsequent sufferings of Mrs. Rachel Plummer (his daughter) during a captivity of twenty-one months among the Comanche Indians, etc. 18 mo, p. p. 95—35, boards. Louisville, 1844.

plentifully in that elevated and delightful region, so long inhabited by the lordly Comanches.

When just arrived at manhood, John accompanied a raiding party down the Rio Grande and into Mexico. Among the captives taken was a young Mexican girl of great beauty, to whom the young warrior felt his heart go out. The affection was reciprocated on the part of the fair Dona Juanita, and the two were soon engaged to be married, so soon as they should arrive at the Comanche village. Each day as the cavalcade moved leisurely, but steadily along, the lovers could be seen riding together, and discussing the anticipated pleasures of connubial life, when suddenly John was prostrated by a violent attack of smallpox. The cavalcade could not tarry, and so it was decided that the poor fellow should be left all alone in the vast *Llano Esticado* to die or recover as fate decreed. But the little Aztec beauty refused to leave her lover, insisting on her captors allowing her to remain and take care of him. To this the Indians reluctantly consented.

With Juanita to nurse and cheer him up, John lingered, lived, and ultimately recovered, when, with as little ceremony, perhaps, as consummated the nuptials of the first pair in Eden, they assumed the matrimonial relation; and Dona Juanita's predilections for the customs and comforts of civilization were sufficiently strong to induce her lord to abandon the wild and nomadic life of a savage for the comforts to be found in a straw-thatched *Jackal*.

"They settled," says Mr. Thrall, the historian of Texas, "on a stock ranch in the far West."

When the civil war broke out John Parker joined a Mexican company in the Confederate service, and was noted for his gallantry and daring. He, however, refused to leave the soil of Texas, and would, under no circumstances, cross the Sabine into Louisiana. He was still living on his ranch across the Rio Grande a few years ago, but up to that time had never visited any of his relatives in Texas.

Of Cynthia Ann Parker (we will anticipate the thread of the narrative). Four long years have elapsed since she was cruelly torn from a mother's embrace and carried into captivity. During this time no tidings have been received of her. Many efforts have been made to ascertain her whereabouts, or fate, but without success; when in 1840, Col. Len. Williams, an old and honoured Texian, Mr. —— Stoat, a trader, and a Delaware Indian guide, named "Jack Harry," packed mules with goods and engaged in an expedition of private traffic with the Indians.

On the Canadian River they fell in with Pa-ha-u-ka's band of Comanches, with whom they were peaceably conversant. And with this tribe was Cynthia Ann Parker, who from the day of her capture had never seen a white person. She was then about fourteen years of age and had been with the Indians nearly five years.

Col. Williams found the Indian into whose family she had been adopted, and proposed to redeem her, but the Comanche told him all the goods he had would not ransom her, and at the same time "the fierceness of his countenance," says Col. Williams, "warned me of the danger of further mention of the subject." But old Pa-ha-u-ka prevailed upon him to let them see her. She came and sat down by the root of a tree, and while their presence was doubtless a happy event to the poor stricken captive, who in her doleful captivity had endured everything but death, she refused to speak a word.

As she sat there, musing, perhaps, of distant relatives and friends, and the bereavements at the beginning and progress of her distress, they employed every persuasive art to evoke some expression. They told her of her playmates and relatives, and asked what message she would send them, but she had doubtless been commanded to silence, and with no hope or prospect of return was afraid to appear sad or dejected, and by a stoical effort in order to prevent future bad treatment, put the best face possible on the matter. But the anxiety of her mind was betrayed by the perceptible quiver of her lips, showing that she was not insensible to the common feelings of humanity.

As the years rolled by Cynthia Ann speedily developed the charms of womanhood, as with the dusky maidens of her companionship she performed the menial offices of drudgery to which savage custom consigns women,—or practiced those little arts of coquetry maternal to the female heart, whether she be a *belle* of Madison Square, attired in the most elaborate toilet from the *élite* bazaars of Paris, or the half naked savage with matted locks and claw-like nails.

Doubtless the heart of more than one warrior was pierced by the Ulyssean darts from her laughing eyes, or charmed by the silvery ripple of her joyous laughter, and laid at her feet the game taken after a long and arduous chase among the Antelope Hills.

Among the number whom her budding charms brought to her shrine was Peta Nocona. a Comanche war chief, in prowess and renown the peer of the famous and redoubtable "Big Foot," who fell in a desperately contested hand-to-hand encounter with the veteran ranger and Indian fighter, Captain S. P. Ross, now living at Waco, and whose wonderful exploits and deeds of daring furnished themes for song and story at the war dance, the council, and the camp-fire.

Cynthia Ann,—stranger now to every word of her mother tongue save her own name became the bride of Pata Nocona, performing for her imperious lord all the slavish offices which savageism and Indian custom assigns as the duty of a wife. She bore him children, and we are assured *loved* him with a species of fierce passion, and wifely devotion; "for some fifteen years after her capture," says Victor M. Rose, "a party of white hunters, including some friends of her family, visited the Comanche encampment on the upper Canadian, and recognizing Cynthia Ann—probably through the medium of her name alone, sounded her in a secret manner as to the disagreeableness of a return to her people and the haunts of civilization.

She shook her head in a sorrowful negative, and pointed to her little, naked barbarians sporting at her feet, and to the great greasy, lazy buck sleeping in the shade near at hand, the locks of a score of scalps dangling at his belt, and whose first utterance upon arousing would be a stern command to his meek, pale-faced wife. Though in truth, exposure to sun and air had browned the complexion of Cynthia Ann almost as intensely as were those of the native daughters of the plains and forest.

She retained but the vaguest remembrance of her people—as dim and flitting as the phantoms of a dream; she was accustomed now to the wild life she led, and found in its repulsive features charms which "upper tendom" would have proven totally deficient in:—"I am happily wedded," she said to these visitors. "I love my husband, who is good and kind, and my little ones, who, too, are his, and I cannot forsake them!"

What were the incidents in the savage life of these children which in after times became the land marks in the train of memory, and which with civilized creatures serves as incentives to reminiscence?

"Doubtless," says Mr. Rose, "Cynthia Ann arrayed herself in the calico borne from the sacking of Linville, and fled with the discomfited Comanches up the Gaudaloupe and Colorado, at the ruthless march of John H. Moore, Ben McCulloch and their hardy rangers. They must have been present at the battle of Antelope Hills, on the Canadian, when Col. John S. Ford, "Old Rip" and Captain S. P. Ross encountered the whole force of the Comanches, in 1858; perhaps John Parker was an actor in that celebrated battle; and again at the Wichita."

"Theirs must have been a hard and unsatisfactory life the Comanches are veritable Ishmaelites, their hands being raised against all men, and every man's hand against them. Literally, *eternal vigilance was the price of liberty* with them, and of life itself. Every night the dreaded surprise was sought to be guarded against; and every copse was scanned for the anticipated ambuscade while upon the march. Did they flout the blood-drabbled scalps of helpless whites in fiendish glee, and assist at the cruel torture of the unfortunate prisoners that fell into their hands? Alas! forgetful of their race and tongue, they were thorough savages, and acted in all particulars just as their Indian comrades did. Memory was stored but with the hard ships and the cruelties of the life about them; arid the stolid indifference of mere animal existence furnishes no finely wrought springs for the rebound of reminiscence."

★ ★ ★ ★ ★ ★ ★ ★

The year 1846, one decade from the fall of Parker's Fort, witnessed the end of the Texian Republic, in whose councils Isaac Parker served as a senator, and the blending of the *Lone Star* with the galaxy of the great constellation of the American Union—during which time many efforts were made to ascertain definitely the whereabouts of the captives, as an indispensable requisite to their reclamation sometimes by solitary scouts and spies, sometimes through the medium of negotiation and sometimes by waging direct war against their captors,—but all to no avail.

★ ★ ★ ★ ★ ★ ★ ★

Another decade passes away, and the year 1856 arrives. The hardy pioneers have pushed the frontier of civilization far to the north and west, driving the Indian and the buffalo before them. The scene of Parker's Fort is now in the heart of a dense population; farms, towns, churches, and school houses lie along the path by which the Indians marched from their camp at the "water-hole" in that bloody May of 1836, Isaac Parker is now a Representative in the Legislature of the State of Texas. It is now twenty years since the battle of San Jacinto twenty years since John and Cynthia Ann were borne into a captivity worse than death the last gun of the Mexican war rung out its last report over the conquered capital of Mexico ten long years ago; but John and Cynthia Ann Parker have sent no tokens to their so long anxious friends that they even live: Alas! time even blunts the edge of anxiety, and sets bounds alike to the anguish of man, as well as to his hopes.

The punishment of Prometheas is not of this world!

CHAPTER 3

THE BATTLE OF ANTELOPE HILLS

Brave Colonel Ford the commander and ranger bold,
On the South Canadian did the Comanches behold,
On the 12th of May, at rising of sun,
The armies did meet and the battle begun.

The battle of the South Canadian or "Antelope Hills," fought in 1858, was probably one of the most splendid scenic exhibitions of Indian warfare ever en acted upon Texas soil. This was the immemorial home of the Comanches here they sought refuge from their marauding expeditions into Texas and Mexico; and here, in their veritable "city of refuge," should the adventurous and daring rangers seek them, it was certain that they would be encountered in full force—Pohebits Quasho—"Iron Jacket," so called from the fact that he wore a coat of scale mail, a curious piece of ancient armour, which doubtless had been stripped from the body of some unfortunate Spanish Knight slain, perhaps, a century before—some *chevalier* who followed Coronado, De Leon, La Salle—was the war chief. He was a "Big Medicine" man, or Prophet, and claimed to be invulnerable to balls and arrows aimed at his person, as by a necromantic puff of his breath the missives were diverted from their course, or charmed, and made to fall harmless at his feet.

Peta Nocono, the young and daring husband of Cynthia Ann Parker, was second in command.

About the 1st of May, in the year above named, Col. John S. Ford, ("Old Rip,") at the head of 100 Texian Rangers—comprising such leaders as Capts. S. P. Ross, (the father of Gen. L. S. Ross); W. A. Pitts, Preston, Tankersley, and a contingent of 111 Toncahua Indians, the latter commanded by their celebrated chief, Placido—so long the faithful and implicitly trusted friend of the whites—marched on a campaign against the marauding Comanches, determined to follow them up to their stronghold amid the hills of the Canadian river, and if possible surprise them and inflict a severe and lasting chastisement.

After a toilsome march of several days the Toncahua scouts reported that they were in the immediate vicinity of the Comanche encampment. The Comanches, though proverbial for their sleepless vigilance, were unsuspicious of danger and so unsuspected was the approach of the rangers, that on the day preceding the battle, Col. Ford and Capt. Ross stood in the old road from Fort Smith to Santa Fe, just north of the Rio Negro or "False Wichita," and watched through their glasses the Comanches running buffalo in the valleys still more to the north. That night the Toncahua spies completed the hazardous mission of locating definitely the position of the enemy's encampment. The next morning (May 12) the rangers and "reserve" or friendly Indians, marched before sunrise to the attack.

Placido claimed for his "red warriors" the privilege of wreaking vengeance upon their hereditary enemies. His request was granted,- and the Toncahuas effected a complete surprise. The struggle was short, sharp and sanguinary. The women and children were made prisoners, but not a Comanche brave surrendered. Their savage pride preferred death to the restraints and humiliations of captivity. Not a single warrior escaped to bear the sorrowful tidings of this destructive engagement to their people.

A short time after the sun had lighted the tops of the hills, the rangers came in full view of the hostile camp, pitched in one of the picturesque valleys of the Canadian, and on the opposite side of the stream, in the immediate vicinity of the famous "Antelope Hills."

The panorama thus presented to the view of the rangers was beautiful in the extreme, and their pent-up enthusiasm found vent in a shout of exultation, which was speedily suppressed by Col. Ford. Just at this moment a solitary Comanche was descried riding southward, evidently heading for the village which Placido had so recently destroyed. He was wholly unconcious of the proximity of an enemy. Instant pursuit was now made; he turned, and fled at full speed toward the main camp across the Canadian, closely followed by the rangers.

He dashed across the stream, and thus revealed to his pursuers the locality of a safe ford across the miry and almost impassable river. He rushed into the village beyond, sounding the notes of alarm; and soon the Comanche warriors presented a bold front of battle-line between their women and children and the advancing rangers. After a few minutes occupied in forming line of battle, both sides were arrayed in full force and effect. The friendly Indians were placed on the right, and thrown a little forward. Col. Ford's object was to deceive the Comanches as to the character of the attacking force, and as to the quality of arms they possessed.

Pohebits Quasho, arrayed in all the trappings of his "war toggery"-coat of mail, shield, bow and lance, completed by a head-dress decorated with feathers and long red flannel streamers; and besmeared in "war paint,"—gaily dashed about on his "war-horse" mid way of the opposing lines, delivering taunts and challenges to the whites. As the old chief dashed to and fro a number of rifles were discharged at him in point blank range without any effect whatever; which seeming immunity to death encouraged his warriors greatly; and induced even some of the more superstitious among the rangers to enquire within themselves if it were possible that "Old Iron Jacket" really bore a charmed life?

Followed by a few of his braves, he now bore down upon the rangers, described a few "charmed circles," gave a few necromantic puffs with his breath and let fly several arrows at Col. Ford, Capt. Ross and chief Placido; receiving their fire without harm. But as he approached the line of the Toncahuas, a rifle directed by the steady nerve and unerring eye of one of their number, Jim Pockmark, brought the "Big Medicine" to the dust. The shot was a mortal one. The fallen chieftain was instantly surrounded by his braves, but the spirit of the conjuring brave had taken its flight to the "happy hunting grounds."

These incidents occupied but a brief space of time, when the order to charge was given; and then ensued one of the grandest assaults ever made against the Comanches. The enthusiastic shouts of the rangers and the triumphant yell of their red allies greeted the welcome order. It was responded to by the defiant "war-hoop" of the Comanches, and in those virgin hills, remote from civilization, the saturnalia of battle was inaugurated. The shouts of enraged combatants, the wail of women, the piteous cries of terrified children, the howling of frightened dogs, the deadly reports of rifle and revolver, constituted a discordant confusion of sounds, blent together in an unearthly mass of infernal noise.

The conflict was sharp and quick—a charge; a momentary exchange of rifle and arrow shots, and the heart-rending wail of discomfiture and dismay, and the beaten Comanches abandoned their lodges and camp to the victors, and began a disorderly retreat. But sufficient method was observed to take advantage of each grove of timber, each hill and ravine, to make a stand against their pursuers; and thus enable the women and children to make their escape. The noise of battle now diverged from a common centre like the spokes of a wheel, and continued to greet the ear for several hours, gradually growing fainter as the pursuit disappeared in the distance.

But another division, under the vigilant Peta Nocona, was soon marching through the hills north of the Canadian, to the rescue. Though ten miles distant, his quick ear had caught the first sounds of the battle; and soon he was riding, with Cynthia Ann by his side, at the head of (500) five hundred warriors.

About 1 o'clock of the afternoon the last of the rangers returned from the pursuit of Pohebits Quasho's discomfited braves, just in time to anticipate this threatened attack.

As Capt. Ross (who was one of the last to return) rode up, he enquired "What hour of the morning is it, Colonel?"

"Morning!" exclaimed Col. Ford, "it is one o'clock of the afternoon;" so unconscious is one of the flight of time during an engagement, that the work of hours seems comprised within the space of a few moments.

"Hello! what are you in line of battle for?" asked Ross. "Look at the hills there, and you will see," calmly replied Col. Ford, pointing to the hills some half a mile distant, behind which the forces of Peta Nocona were visible; an imposing line of 500 warriors drawn up in battle array.

Col. Ford had with 221 men fought and routed over 400 Comanches, and now he was confronted by a stronger force, fresh from their village still higher up on the Canadian. They had come to drive the "pale faces" and their hated copper-coloured allies from the captured camp, to retake prisoners, to retake over four hundred head of horses and an immense quantity of plunder. They did not fancy the defiant state of preparations awaiting them in the valley, however, and were waiting to avail themselves of some incautious movement on the part of the rangers, when the wily Peta Nocona with his forces would spring like a lion from his lair, and with one combined and desperate effort swoop down and annihilate the enemy. But his antagonist was a soldier of too much sagacity to allow any advantage to a vigilant foe.

The two forces remained thus contemplating each other for over an hour; during which time a series of operations ensued between single combatants illustrative of the Indian mode of warfare, and the marked difference between the nomadic Comanche and his semi-civilized congeners, the Tonchua. The Tonchuas took advantage of ravines, trees and other natural shelter. Their arms were rifles and "six-shooters." The Comanches came to the attack with shield and bow and lance, mounted on gaily caparisoned and prancing steeds, and flaunting feathers and all the "gorgeous" display incident to savage "finery" and pomp. They are probably the most expert equestrians in the world. A Comanche warrior would gaily canter to a point half way between the opposing lines, yell a defiant "war hoop," and shake his shield. This was a challenge to single combat.

Several of the friendly Indians who accepted such challenges were placed *hors de combat* by their more expert adversaries, and in consequence Col. Ford ordered them to decline the savage banters; much to the dissatisfaction of Placido, who had conducted himself throughout the series of engagements with the bearing of a savage hero.

Says Col. Ford: "In these combats the mind of the spectator was vividly carried back to the days of chivalry; the jousts and tournaments of knights and to the concomitants of those scenic exhibitions of gallantry. The feats of horsemanship were splendid, the lances and shields were used with great dexterity, and the whole performance was a novel show to civilized man."

Col. Ford now ordered Placido, with a part of his warriors, to advance in the direction of the enemy, and if possible draw them in the valley, so as to afford the rangers an opportunity to charge them. This had the desired effect, and the rangers were ready to deliver a charge, when it was discovered that the friendly Indians had removed the white badges from their heads because they served as targets for the Comanches, consequently the rangers were unable to distinguish friend from foe. This necessitated the entire withdrawal of the Indians. The Comanches witnessed these preparations and now commenced to recoil. The rangers advanced; the trot, the gallop, the headlong charge, followed in rapid succession. Lieut. Nelson made a skilful movement and struck the enemy's left flank.

The Comanche line was broken. A running fight for three or four miles ensued. The enemy was driven back wherever he made a stand. The most determined resistance was made in a timbered ravine. Here one of Placido's warriors was killed, and one of the rangers, young George W. Pascal wounded. The Comanches left some dead upon the spot and had several more wounded. After routing them at this point the rangers continued to pursue them some distance, intent upon taking the women and children prisoners but Peta Nocona, by the exercise of those commanding qualities which had often before signalized his conduct on the field, succeeded in covering their retreat, and thus al lowing them to escape. It was now about 4 p. m., both horses and men were almost entirely exhausted, and Col. Ford ordered a halt and returned to the village.

Brave old Placido and his warriors fought like so many demons. It was difficult to restrain them, so anxious were they to wreak vengeance on the Comanches.

In all of these engagements seventy-five Comanches "bit the dust."

The loss of the rangers was small,—two killed and five or six wounded.

The trophies of Pohebits Quasho, including his lance, bow, shield, head-dress and the celebrated coat of scale mail, was deposited by Col. Ford in the State archives at Austin, where, doubtless, they may yet be seen,—as curious relics of by-gone days.

The lamented old chief, Placido, fell a victim to the revengeful Comanches during the latter part of the great civil war, between the North and South; being assassinated by a party of his enemies on the reservation, near Fort Sill.

The venerable John Henry Brown, some years since, paid a merited tribute to his memory through the columns of the Dallas *Herald*.

Of Placido it has been said that he was the "soul of honour," and "never betrayed a trust." That he was brave to the utmost, we have only to refer to his numerous exploits during his long and gratuitous service on our frontiers. He was implicitly trusted by Burleson and other partisan leaders; and rendered in valuable services in behalf of the early Texian pioneers; in recognition of which he never received any reward of a material nature, beyond a few paltry pounds of gunpowder and salt. Imperial Texas should rear a monument commemorative of his memory. He was the more than Tammany of Texas! But I am digressing from the narrative proper.

"Doubtless," says Rose, "Cynthia Ann rode from this ill-starred field with her infant daughter pressed to her bosom, and her sons-two youths of about ten and twelve years of age, at her side,—as fearful of capture at the hands of the hated whites, as years ago immediately after the massacre of Parker's Fort—she had been anxious for the same."

CHAPTER 4
GENL. L. S. ROSS.—BATTLE OF THE WICHITA

It is not our purpose in this connection, to assume the role of biographer to so distinguished a personage as is the chevalier Bayard of Texas—General Lawrence Sullivan Ross. That task should be left to an abler pen; and besides, it would be impossible to do anything like justice to the romantic, adventurous, and altogether splendid and brilliant career of the brave and daring young ranger who rescued Cynthia Ann Parker from captivity, at least in the circumscribed limits of a brief biographical sketch, such as we shall be compelled to confine ourselves to; yet, some brief mention of his services and exploits as a ranger captain, by way of an introduction to the reader beyond the limits of Texas, where his name and fame are as household words, is deemed necessary, hence we beg leave here to give a brief sketch of his life.

"Texas, though her annals be brief," says the author of *Ross' Texas Brigade*, "counts upon her 'roll of honour' the names of many heroes, living and dead. Their splendid services are the inestimable legacies of the past and present, to the future. Of the latter, it is the high prerogative of the State to embalm their names and memories as perpetual examples to excite the generous emulation of the Texian youth to the latest posterity. Of the former it is our pleasant province to accord them those honours which their services, in so eminent a degree, entitle them to receive. Few lands, since the days of the 'Scottish Chiefs,' have furnished material upon which to predicate a Douglas, a Wallace, or a Ravenswood; and the adventures of chivalric enterprise, arrant quest of danger, and the personal combat, were relegated, together with the knight's armorial trappings, to the rusty archives of 'Tower' and 'Pantheon, ' until the Comanche Bedouins of the Texian plains tendered in bold defiance the savage gauntlet to the pioneer knights of progress and civilization. And though her heraldic roll glows with the names of a Houston, a Rusk, Lamar, McCulloch, Hayes, Chevellie, which illumine the pages of her history with an effulgence of glory, Texas never nurtured on her maternal bosom a son of more filial devotion, of more loyal patriotism, or indomitable will to do and dare, than L. S. Ross."

Lawrence Sullivan Ross was born in the village of Bentonsport, Ohio, in the year 1838. His father, Captain S.. P. Ross, emigrated to Texas in 1839, casting his fortunes with the struggling pioneers who were blazing the pathway of civilization into the wilds of a *terra incognita*, as Texas then was.

"Captain S. P. Ross was, for many years, pre-eminent as a leader against the implacable savages, who made frequent incursions into the settlements. The duty of repelling these forays usually devolved upon Captain Ross and his neighbours, and, for many years, his company constituted the only bulwark of safety between the feeble colonist and the scalping knife. The rapacity and treachery of his Comanche and Kiowa foes demanded of Captain Ross sleepless vigilance, acute sagacity, and a will that brooked no obstacle or danger. It was in the performance of this arduous duty that he slew, in single combat, 'Big Foot,' a Comanche chief of great prowess, and who was for many years the scourge of the early Texas frontier. The services of Captain S. P. Ross are still held in grateful remembrance by the descendants of his compatriots, and his memory will never be suffered to pass away while Texians feel a pride in the sterling worth of the pioneers who laid the foundation of Texas' greatness and glory."—*Vide Ross' Texas Brigade.*

The following incident, as illustrative of the character and spirit of the man and times, is given:

On one occasion, Captain Ross, who had been visiting a neighbour, was returning home, afoot, accompanied by his little son, 'Sul,' as the general was familiarly called. When within half a mile of his house, he was surrounded by fifteen or twenty mounted Comanche warriors, who commenced an immediate attack. The captain, athletic and swift of foot, threw his son on his back, and outran their ponies to the house, escaping unhurt amid a perfect shower of arrows.

Such were among the daily experiences of the child, and with such impressions stamped upon the infantile mind, it was but natural that the enthusiastic spirit of the ardent youth should lead him to such adventures upon the "war-path," similar to those that had signalized his honoured father's prowess upon so many occasions.

Hence, we find "Sul" Ross, during vacation from his studies at Florence Weslean University, Alabama, though a beardless boy, scarcely twenty years of age, in command of a contingent of 135 friendly Indians, co-operating with the United States cavalry under the dashing Major Earl Van Dorn, in a campaign against the Comanches.

★ ★ ★ ★ ★ ★ ★ ★

Notwithstanding the severe chastisement that had been inflicted on the Comanches at "Antelope Hills," they soon renewed their hostilities, committing many depredations and murders during the summer of 1858.

Early in September Major Van Dorn received orders from Gen. Twiggs, to equip four companies, including Ross' "red warriors," and go out on a scouting expedition against the hostile Indians. This he did, penetrating the heart of the Indian country where he proceeded to build a stockade, placing within it all the pack mules, extra horses and supplies, which was left in charge of the infantry.

Ross' faithful Indian scouts soon reported the discovery of a large Comanche village near the Wichita Mountains, about ninety miles away. The four companies, attended by the spies, immediately set out for the village, and after a fatiguing march of thirty-six hours, causing the men to be continuously in the saddle the latter sixteen hours of the ride, arrived in the immediate vicinity of the Indian camp just at daylight on the morning of October 1st.

A reconnoissance showed that the wily Comanches were not apprehensive of an attack, and were sleeping in fancied security. The horses of the tribe, which consisted of a *caballado* of about 500 head, were grazing near the outskirts of the village. Major Van Dorn directed Captain Ross, at the head of his Indians, to "round up" the horses, and drive them from the camp, which was effected speedily, and thus the Comanches were forced to fight on foot—a proceeding extremely harrowing to the proud warriors' feelings.

Just as the sun was peeping above the eastern horizon," says Victor M. Rose, whose graphic narrative we again quote, "Van Dorn charged the upper end of the village, while Ross' command, in conjunction with a detachment of United States cavalry, charged the lower. The village was strung out along the banks of a branch for several hundred yards. The morning was very foggy, and after a few moments of firing the smoke and fog became so dense that objects at but a short distance could be distinguished only with great difficulty. The Comanches fought with absolute desperation, and contended for every advantage, as their women and children, and all their possessions, were in peril.

A few moments after the engagement became general, Ross discovered a number of Comanches running down to the branch, about one hundred and fifty yards from the village, and concluded that they were beating a retreat. Immediately, Ross, Lieutenant Van Camp of the United States Army, Alexander, a 'regular' soldier, and one Caddo Indian, of Ross' command, ran to the point with the intention of intercepting them. Arriving, it was discovered that the fugitives were the women and children. In a moment, another posse of women and children came running immediately past the squad of Ross, who, discovering a little white girl among the number, made his Caddo Indian grab her as she was passing. The little pale-face—apparently about twelve years of age—was badly frightened at finding herself a captive to a strange Indian and stranger white men, and was hard to manage at first.

Ross now discovered, through the fog and smoke of the battle, that a band of some twenty-five Comanche warriors had cut his small party off from communication with Van Dorn, and were bearing immediately down upon them. They shot Lieutenant Van Camp through the heart, killing him ere he could fire his double-barrelled shot-gun. Alexander, the United States Cavalryman, was likewise shot down before he could fire his gun (a rifle). Ross was armed with a Sharp's rifle, and attempted to fire upon the exultant red devils, but the cap snapped. 'Mohee,' a Comanche warrior, seized Alexander's rifle and shot Ross down.

The indomitable young ranger fell upon the side on which his pistol was borne, and though partially paralyzed by the shot, he turned himself, and was getting his pistol out when 'Mohee' drew his butcher-knife, and started towards his prostrate foe—some fifteen feet away—with the evident design of stabbing and scalping him. He made but a few steps, however, when one of his companions cried out something in the Comanche tongue, which was a signal to the band, and they broke away in confusion.

'Mohee' ran about twenty steps, when a wire-cartridge, containing nine buck-shot, fired from a gun in the hands of Lieutenant James Majors, (afterwards a Confederate General), struck him between the shoulders, and he fell forward on his face, dead. 'Mohee' was an old acquaintance of Ross, as the latter had seen him frequently at his father's post on the frontier, and recognized him as soon as their eyes met. The faithful Caddo held on to the little girl throughout this desperate *mêlée*, and,

GENERAL L S ROSS.

strange to relate, neither were harmed. The Caddo, doubtless, owed his escape to the fact that the Comanches were fearful of wounding or killing the little girl.

This whole scene transpired in a few moments, and Captain N. G. Evans' company of the Second United States Cavalry, had taken possession of the lower end of the Comanche village, and Major Van Dorn held the upper, and the Comanches were running into the hills and brush; not, however, before an infuriated Comanche shot the gallant Van Dorn with an arrow. Van Dorn fell, and it was supposed that he was mortally wounded. In consequence of their wounds, the two chieftains were compelled to remain on the battle ground five or six days.

After the expiration of this time, Ross' Indians made a 'litter,' after their fashion, borne between two gentle mules, and in it placed their heroic and beloved 'boy captain,' and set out for the settlements at Fort Belknap. When this mode of conveyance would become too painful, by reason of the rough, broken nature of the country, these brave Caddos—whose race and history are but synonyms of courage and fidelity—would vie with each other in bearing the burden upon their own shoulders. At Camp Radziminski, occupied by United States forces, an ambulance was obtained, and the remainder of the journey made with comparative comfort. Major Van Dorn was also conveyed to Radziminski. He speedily recovered of his wound, and soon made another brilliant campaign against the Comanches, as we shall see further on. Ross recovered sufficiently in a few weeks so as to be able to return to college at Florence, Alabama, where he completed his studies, and graduated in 1859.

This was the battle of the Wichita Mountains, a hotly contested and most desperate hand to hand fight in which the two gallant and dashing young officers, Ross and Van Dorn, were severely wounded. The loss of the whites was five killed and several wounded.

The loss of the Comanches was, eighty or ninety warriors killed, many wounded, and several captured; besides losing all their horses, camp equipage, supplies, etc.

The return of this victorious little army was hailed with enthusiastic rejoicing and congratulation, and the Wichita fight and Van Dorn and Ross were the themes of song and story for many years along the borders and in the halls and banqueting-rooms of the cities, and the martial music of the "Wichita March" resounded through the plains of Texas wherever the Second Cavalry encamped or rode off on scouts in after years.

The little girl captive of whose parentage or history nothing could be ascertained, though strenuous efforts were made was christened "Lizzie Ross," in honour of Miss *Lizzie* Tinsley, daughter of Dr. D. R. Tinsley, of Waco, to whom Ross at that time was engaged; and afterwards married—May, 1861.

Of Lizzie Ross, it can be said that, in her career, is afforded a thorough verification of Lord Byron's saying: *Truth is stranger than fiction!* She was adopted by her brave and generous captor, properly reared and educated, and became a beautiful and accomplished woman. Here were sufficient romance and vicissitude, in the brief career of a little maiden, to have turned the "roundelay's" of "troubadour and *meunesauger.*" A solitary lily, blooming amidst the wildest grasses of the desert plains. A little Indian girl in all save the Caucasian's conscious stamp of superiority. Torn from home, perhaps, amid the heart rending scenes of rapine, torture and death. A stranger to race and lineage—stranger even to the tongue in which a mother's lullaby was breathed. Affiliating with these wild Ishmaelites of the prairie—a Comanche in all things save the intuitive premonition *that she was not of them!* Finally, redeemed from a captivity worse than death by a knight entitled to rank, for all time in the history of Texas, "*primus inter pores*"—*Vide Ross Texas Brigade.*

Lizzie Ross accompanied Gen. Ross' mother on a visit to the State of California, a few years since, and while there, became the wife of a wealthy merchant near Los Angeles, where she now resides.

Such is the romantic story of "Lizzie Ross"—a story that derives additional interest because of the fact of its absolute truth in all respects.

★ ★ ★ ★ ★ ★ ★ ★ ★

The following letter from Gen. L. S. Ross, touching upon the battle of the Wichita Mountains and the recapture of "Lizzie Ross," is here appropriately inserted:

Waco, Texas, July 12. 1884.

Mr. James T. Deshields. Dear Sir:—My father could give you reliable data enough to fill a volume. I send you photograph of Cynthia Ann Parker, with notes relating to her on back of photo. On the 28th of October, 1858, I had a battle with the

Comanches at Wichita Mts., and there recaptured a little white girl about eight years old, whose parentage, nor indeed any trace of her kindred, was ever found. I adopted, reared, and educated her, giving her the name of Lizzie Ross; the former name being in honour of the young lady—Lizzie Tinsley—to whom I was then engaged and afterwards married—May, 1861.

Lizzie Ross grew to womanhood, and married a wealthy merchant living near Los Angeles, California, where she now resides. See *History of 'Ross' Brigade* by Victor M. Rose, and published by *Courier-Journal*, for a full and graphic description of the battle and other notable incidents. I could give you many interesting as well as thrilling adventures of self and father's family with the Indians in the early settlement of the country.

He can give you more information than any living Texian, touching the Indian character, having been their agent and warm and trusted friend, in whom they had confidence.

My early life was one of constant danger from their forays, and I was twice in their hands and at their mercy, as well as the other members of my father's family.

But I am just now too busy with my farm matters to give you such data as would subserve your purpose.

Yours truly,   L. S. Ross.

CHAPTER 5
BATTLE OF PEASE RIVER—CYNTHIA ANN PARKER

For some time after Ross' victory at the Wichita Mountains the Comanches were less hostile, seldom penetrating far down into the settlements. But in 1859-'60 the condition of the frontier was again truly deplorable. The people were obliged to stand in a continued posture of defence, and were in continual alarm and hazard of their lives, never daring to stir abroad unarmed, for small bodies of savages, quick-sighted and accustomed to perpetual watchfulness, hovered on the outskirts, and springing from behind bush or rock, surprised his enemy before he was aware of danger, and sent tidings of his presence in the fatal blow, and after execution of the bloody work, by superior knowledge of the country and rapid movements, safely retired to their inaccessible deserts.

In the Autumn of 1860 the indomitable and fearless Peta Nocona led a raiding party of Comanches through Parker county, so named in honour of the family of his wife, Cynthia Ann, committing great depredations as they passed through. The venerable Isaac Parker was at the time a resident of the town of Weatherford, the county seat; and little did he imagine that the chief of the ruthless savages who spread desolation and death on every side as far as their arms could reach , was the husband of his long lost niece and that the comingled blood of the murdered Parkers and the atrocious Comanche now coursed in the veins of a second generation—bound equally by the ties of consanguinity to murderer and murdered; that the son of Peta Nocona and Cynthia Ann Parker would become the chief of the proud Comanches, whose boast it is that their constitutional settlement of government is the purest democracy ever originated and administered among men. It certainly conserved the object of its institution—the protection and happiness of the people—for a longer period, and much more satisfactorily than has that of any other Indian tribe.

The Comanches claimed a superiority over the other Texian tribes and they unquestionably were more intelligent and courageous. The "Reservation Policy,"—necessary though it be—brings them all to an object level,—the plane of lazy beggars and thieves. The Comanche is the most qualified by nature for receiving education and for adapting himself to the requirements of civilization, of all the southern tribes, not excepting even the Cherokees, with their churches, school-houses and farms. The Comanches after waging an unceasing war for nearly fifty years against the United States, Texas and Mexico, still number 16,000 souls; a far better showing than any other tribe can make, though not one but has enjoyed privileges to which the Comanche was a stranger. It is a shame to the civilization of the age that a people so susceptible of a high degree of development should be allowed to grovel in the depths of heathenism and savagery. But we are digressing.

The loud and clamorous cries of the settlers along the frontier for protection, induced the Government to organize and send out a regiment under Col. M. T. Johnson to take the field for public defence. But these efforts proved of small service. The expedition, though at great expense to the state, failed to find an Indian until returning, the command was followed by the wily Comanches, their horses "stampeded" at night and most of the men compelled to reach the settlements on foot, under great suffering and exposure.

Captain "Sul" Ross, who had just graduated from Florence Wesleyan University, of Alabama, and re turned to Texas, was commissioned a captain of rangers, by Governor Sam Houston, and directed to organize a company of sixty men, with orders to repair to Fort Belknap, receive from Col. Johnson all government property, as his regiment was disbanded, and take the field against the redoubtable Peta Nocona, and afford the frontier such protection as was possible to this small force. The necessity of vigorous measures soon became so pressing that Capt. Ross determined to attempt to curb the insolence of these implacable enemies of Texas by following them into their fastnesses and carry the war into their own homes. In his graphic narration of this campaign Gen. L. S. Ross says:

As I could take but forty of my men from my post, I requested Capt. N. G. Evans, in command of the United States troops, at Camp Cooper, to send me a detachment of the Second Cavalry. We had been intimately connected on the Van Dorn campaign, during which I was the recipient of much kindness from Capt. Evans while I was suffering from a severe wound received from an Indian in the Battle of the 'Wichita.' He promptly sent me a sergeant and twenty well mounted men. My force was still further augmented by some seventy volunteer citizens under command of the brave old frontiersman, Capt. Jack Cureton, of Bosque county. These self-sacrificing patriots, without the hope of pay or reward, left their defenceless homes and families to avenge the sufferings of the frontier people. With pack-mules laden down with necessary supplies the expedition marched for the Indian country.

On the 18th of December, 1860, while marching up Pease River, I had some suspicions that Indians were in the vicinity, by reason of the buffalo that came running in great numbers from the north towards us, and while my command moved in the low ground I visited all neighbouring high points to make discoveries. On one of these sand hills I found four fresh pony tracks, and being satisfied that Indian *videtts* had just gone, I galloped forward about a mile to a higher point, and riding to the top, to my inexpressible surprise, found myself within 200 yards of a Comanche village, located on a small stream winding around the base of the hill.

It was a most happy circumstance that a piercing north wind was blowing, bearing with it clouds of sand, and my presence was unobserved and the surprise complete. By signalling my men as I stood concealed, they reached me without being discovered by the Indians, who were busy packing up preparatory to a move. By this time the Indians mounted and moved off north across the level plain. My command, with the detachment of the Second Cavalry, had out-marched and become separated from the citizen command, which left me about sixty men. In making disposition for attack, the sergeant and his twenty men were sent at a gallop, behind a chain of sand hills, to encompass them in and cut off their retreat, while with forty men I charged.

The attack was so sudden that a considerable number were killed before they could prepare for defence. They fled precipitately right into the presence of the sergeant and his men. Here they met with a warm reception, and finding themselves completely encompassed, everyone fled his own way, and was hotly pursued and hard pressed.

The chief of the party, Peta Nocona, a noted warrior of great repute, with a young girl about fifteen years of age mounted on his horse behind him, and Cynthia Ann Parker, with a girl child about two years of age in her arms and mounted on a fleet pony, fled together, while Lieut. Tom. Kelliheir and I pursued them. After running about a mile Killiheir ran up by the side of Cynthia's horse, and I was in the act of shooting when she held up her child and stopped. I kept on after the chief and about a half a mile further, when in about twenty yards of him I fired my pistol, striking the girl (whom I supposed to be a man, as she rode like one, and only her head was visible above the buffalo robe with which she was wrapped) near the heart, killing her instantly, and the same ball would have killed both but for the shield of the chief, which hung down, covering his back.

When the girl fell from the horse she pulled him off also, but he caught on his feet, and before steadying himself, my horse, running at full speed, was very nearly upon top of him, when he was struck with an arrow, which caused him to fall to pitching or 'bucking,' and it was with great difficulty that I kept my saddle, and in the meantime, narrowly escaped several arrows coming in quick succession from the chief's bow. Being at such disadvantage he would have killed me in a few minutes but for a random shot from my pistol (while I was clinging with my left hand to the pommel of my saddle) which broke his right arm at the elbow, completely disabling him.

My horse then became quiet, and I shot the chief twice through the body, whereupon he deliberately walked to a small tree, the only one in sight, and leaning against it, began to sing a wild, weird song. At this time my Mexican servant, who had once been a captive with the Comanches and spoke their language as fluently as his mother tongue, came up, in company with two of my men. I then summoned the chief to surrender, but he promptly treated every overture with contempt, and signalized this declaration with a savage attempt to thrust me with the lance which he held in his left hand. I could only look upon him with pity and admiration. For, deplorable as was his situation, with no chance of escape, his party utterly destroyed, his wife and child captured in his sight, he was undaunted by the fate that awaited him, and as he seemed to prefer death to life, I directed the Mexican to end his misery by a charge of buck shot from the gun which he carried.

Taking up his accoutrements, which I subsequently sent Gov. Houston, to be deposited in the archives at Austin, we rode back to Cynthia Ann and Killiheir, and found him bitterly cursing himself for having run his pet horse so hard after an 'old squaw.' She was very dirty, both in her scanty garments and her person. But as soon as I looked on her face, I said, 'Why, Tom, this is a white woman, Indians do not have blue eyes.' On the way to the village, where my men were assembling with the spoils, and a large *caballado* of 'Indian ponies,' I discovered an Indian boy about nine years of age, secreted in the grass. Expecting to be killed, he began crying, but I made him mount behind me, and carried him along. And when in after years I frequently proposed to send him to his people, he steadfastly refused to go, and died in McLennan county last year.

After camping for the night Cynthia Ann kept crying, and thinking it was caused from fear of death at our hands, I had the Mexican tell her that we recognized her as one of our own people, and would not harm her. She said two of her boys were with her when the fight began, and she was distressed by the fear that they had been killed. It so happened, however, both escaped, and one of them, 'Quanah' is now a chief. The other died some years ago on the plains. I then asked her to give me the history of her life with the Indians, and the circumstances attending her capture by them, which she promptly did in a

Lizzie Ross

very sensible manner.

And as the facts detailed corresponded with the massacre at Parker's Fort, I was impressed with the belief that she was Cynthia Ann Parker. Returning to my post, I sent her and child to the ladies at Cooper, where she could receive the attention her situation demanded, and at the same time dispatched a messenger to Col. Parker, her uncle, near Weatherford, and as I was called to Waco to meet Gov. Houston, I left directions for the Mexican to accompany Col. Parker to Cooper in the capacity of interpreter. When he reached there, her identity was soon discovered to Col. Parker's entire satisfaction and great happiness.

And thus was fought the battle of "Pease River" between a superior force of Comanches under the implacable chief, Peta Nocona on one side, and sixty rangers led by their youthful commander, Capt. L. S. Ross, on the other. Ross, sword in hand, led the furious rush of the rangers; and in the desperate encounter of "war to the knife" which ensued, nearly all the warriors bit the dust.

So signal a victory had never before been gained over the fierce and war-like Comanches and never since that fatal December clay in 1860 have they made any military demonstrations at all commensurate with the fame of their proud campaigns in the past. The great Comanche confederacy was forever broken. The incessant and sanguinary war which had been waged for more than thirty years was now virtually at an end.

The blow was a most decisive one; as sudden and irresistable as a thunder-bolt, and as remorseless and crushing as the hand of Fate.

It was a short but desperate conflict. Victory trembled in the balance. A determined charge, accompanied by a simultaneous fire from the solid phalanx of yelling rangers and the Comanches beat a hasty retreat, leaving many dead and wounded upon the field. Espying the chief and a chosen few riding at full speed, and in a different direction from the other fugitives, from the ill-starred field, Ross quickly pursued. Divining his purpose, the watchful Pete Nocona rode at full speed, but was soon overtaken, when the two chiefs engaged in a personal encounter, which must result in the death of one or the other. Peta Nocona fell, and his last sigh was taken up in mournful wailings on the wings of defeat. Most of the women and children with a few warriors escaped. Many of these perished on the cold and inhospitable plains, in an effort to reach their friends on the head-waters of the Arkansas River.

The immediate fruits of the victory was some four hundred and fifty horses, and their accumulated winter's supply of food. But the incidental fruits are not to be computed on the basis of dollars and cents. The proud spirit of the Comanche was here broken, and to this signal defeat is to be attributed the measurably pacific conduct of these heretofore implacable foes of the white race during the course of the late civil war in the Union, a boon of incalculable value to Texas.

In a letter recognizing the great service rendered the state by Ross in dealing the Comanches this crushing blow, Governor Houston said:

> Your success in protecting the frontier gives me great satisfaction. I am satisfied that with the same opportunities, you would rival, if not excel, the greatest exploits of McCulloch and Hays. Continue to repel, pursue, and punish every body of Indians coming into the State, and the people will not withhold their praise.   Signed: Sam Houston.

CHAPTER 6

CYNTHIA ANN PARKER—QUANAH PARKER

From May 19th, 1836, to December 18th, 1860, was twenty-four years and seven months. Add to this nine years, her age when captured, and at the later date Cynthia Ann Parker was in her thirty-fourth year. During the last ten years of this quarter of a century, which she spent as a captive among the Comanches, no tidings had been received of her. She had long been given up as dead or irretrievably lost to civilization.

Notwithstanding the long lapse of time which had intervened since the Capture of Cynthia Ann Parker, Ross, as he interrogated his "blue eyed" but bronzed captive, more than suspected that she was the veritable "Cynthia Ann Parker," of which he had heard so much from his boyhood. She was dressed in female attire, of course, according to the custom of the Comanches, which being very similar to that of the males, doubtless, gave rise to the erroneous statement that she was dressed in male costume. So sure was Ross of her identity that, as before stated, he at once dispatched a messenger to her uncle, the venerable Isaac Parker; in the meantime placing Cynthia Ann in charge of Mrs. Evans, wife of Capt. N. G. Evans, the commandant at Fort

Cooper, who at once, with commendable benevolence, administered to her necessities.

Upon the arrival of Col. Parker at Fort Cooper, interrogations were made her through the Mexican interpreter, for she remembered not one word of English, respecting her identity; but she had forgotten absolutely everything, apparently, at all connected with her family or past history.

In despair of being able to reach a conclusion, Col. Parker was about to leave, when he said, "The name of my niece was Cynthia Ann." The sound of the once familiar name, doubtless the last lingering memento of the old home at the fort, seemed to touch a responsive chord in her nature, when a sign of intelligence lighted up her countenance, as memory by some mystic inspiration resumed its cunning as she looked up, and patting her breast, said, "Cynthia Ann! Cynthia Ann!" At the awakening of this single spark of reminiscence, the sole gleam in the mental gloom of many years, her countenance brightened with a pleasant smile in place of the sullen expression which habitually characterizes the looks of an Indian restrained of freedom. There was now no longer any doubt as to her identity with the little girl lost and mourned so long. It was in reality Cynthia Ann Parker,—but, O, so changed!

But as savage-like and dark of complexion as she was, Cynthia Ann was still dear to her overjoyed uncle, and was welcomed home by relatives with all the joyous transports with which the prodigal son was hailed upon his miserable return to the parental roof.

As thorough an Indian in manner and looks as if she had been so born, she sought every opportunity to escape, and had to be closely watched for some time. Her uncle carried herself and child to his home, then took them to Austin, where the secession convention was in session. Mrs. John Henry Brown and Mrs. N. C. Raymond interested themselves in her, dressed her neatly, and on one occasion took her into the gallery of the hall while the convention was in session. They soon realized that she was greatly alarmed by the belief that the assemblage was a council of chiefs, sitting in judgement on her life. Mrs. Brown beckoned to her husband, Hon. John Henry Brown, who was a member of the convention, who appeared and succeeded in reassuring her that she was among friends.

Gradually her mother tongue came back, and with it occasional incidents of her childhood, including a recognition of the venerable Mr. Anglin, and perhaps one or two others.

The civil war coming on soon after, which necessitated the resumption of such primitive arts, she learned to spin, weave and to perform the domestic duties. She proved quite an adept in such work, and became a very useful member of the household.

The ruling passion of her bosom seemed to be the maternal instinct, and she cherished the hope that when the war was concluded she would at last succeed in reclaiming her two children who were still with the Indians. But it was written otherwise, and Cynthia Ann and her little "barbarian" were called hence ere "the cruel war was over." She died at her brother's in Anderson county, Texas, in 1864, preceded a short time by her sprightly little daughter, "Prairie Flower."

Thus ended the sad story of a woman far famed along the border.

★ ★ ★ ★ ★ ★ ★ ★

How fared it with the two young orphans we may only imagine. The lot of these helpless ones is too often one of trials, heart-pangs, and want, even among our enlightened people; and it would require a painful recital to follow the children of Peta Nocona and Cynthia Ann Parker from the terrible fight on Pease River, across trackless prairies, and rugged mountain-ways, in the inhospitable month of December, tired, hungry, and carrying a load upon their hearts far heavier than the physical evils which so harshly beset them. Their father was slain, and their mother a captive. Doubtless they were as intent upon her future recovery, during the many years in which they shared the vicissitudes of their people, until the announcement of her death reached them, as her own family had been for her rescue during her quarter of a century of captivity. One of the little sons of Cynthia Ann died some years after her recapture. The other, now known as Capt. Quanah Parker, born as he says in 1854, is the chief of Comanches, on their reservation in the Indian Territory.

Finally, in 1874, the Comanches were forced upon a "reservation," near Fort Sill, to lead the beggarly life of "hooded harlots and blanketed thieves," and it was at this place that the "war-chief" Quanah, learned that it was possible he might secure a photograph of his mother.[1]

---

1. Mr. A. F. Corning was at Fort Worth in 1862, when Cynthia Ann Parker passed through there. He (Mr. C.) prevailed on her to go with him to a daguerreotype gallery (there were no photographs then) and have her picture taken. Mr. Corning still has this daguerreotype, and says it is an excellent likeness of the woman as she looked then. It is now at the Academy of Art, Waco, and several photographs have been taken from it, one of which was sent to Quanah Parker, and another to the writer, from which the frontispiece to this work was engraved.

An advertisement to that effect was inserted in the Fort Worth *Gazette*, when General Ross at once forwarded him a copy. To his untutored mind it seemed that a miracle had been wrought in response to his "paper prayer;" and his exclamations, as he gazed intently and long upon the faithful representation of "Preloch," or Cynthia Ann, were highly suggestive of Cowper's lines on his mother's picture; and we take the liberty of briefly presenting a portion of the same in verse:

My mother! and do my weeping eyes once more
Half doubting—scan thy cherished features o'er?
Yes, 'tis the pictured likeness of my dead mother,
How true to life! It seems to breathe and move;
Fire, love, and sweetness o'er each feature melt;
The face expresses all the spirit felt;
Here, while I gaze within those large, dark eyes,
I almost see the living spirit rise;
While lights and shadows, all harmonious, glow,
And heavenly radiance settles on that brow.
What is the "medicine" I must not know,
Which thus can give to death life's bloom and glow.
O, could the white man's magic art but give
As well the happy power, and bid her live!
My name, me thinks, would be the first to break
The seal of silence, on those lips, and wake
Once more the smile that charmed her gentle face,
As she was wont to fold me in her warm embrace.
Yes, it is she, "Preloch," Nocona's pale-faced bride,
Who rode, a matchless princess, at his side,
'Neath many a bloody moon afar,
O'er tortuous paths devoted alone to war.
Long since she's joined him on that blissful shore,—
Where parting and heart-breakings are no more,—
And since our star with him went down in gloom,
No more to shine above the blighting doom,
'Neath which my people's hopes, alas, are fled,
I, too, but long that silent path to tread,—
A child, to be with her and him again,
Healed every wound an orphan's heart can pain!

Quanah Parker is a Nocone, which means wanderer, but on the capture of his mother, Preloch, and death of his father, Quanah was adopted and cared for by the Cohoites, and when just arrived at manhood, was made chief by his benefactors on account of his bravery. His name before he became a chief was Cepe. He has lived among several tribes of the Comanches. He was at one time with the Cochetaker, or Buffalo Eaters, and was the most influential chief of the Penatakers. Quanah is at present one of the four chiefs of the Cohoites, who each have as many people as he has. The Cohoite Comanches were never on a reservation until 1874, but are today further advanced in civilization than any Indians on the "Comanche reservation." Quanah speaks English, is considerably advanced in civilization, and owns a ranch with considerable live stock and a small farm; wears a citizen's suit, and con forms to the customs of civilization—withal a fine-looking and dignified son of the plains. In 1884, Quanah, in company with two other prominent Comanche chiefs, visited Mexico. In reporting their passage through that city, the San Antonio *Light* thus speaks of them:

> They bear relationship to each other of chief and two subordinates. Quanah Parker is the chief, and as he speaks very good English, they will visit the City of Mexico before they return. They came from Kiowa, Comanche and Wichita Indian Agency, and Parker bears a paper from Indian Agent Hunt that he, Parker, is a son of Cynthia Ann Parker, and is one of the most prominent chiefs of the half-breed Comanche tribe. He is also a successful stock man and farmer. He wears a citizen's suit of black, neatly fitting, regular "toothpick" dude shoes, a watch and gold chain and black felt hat. The only peculiar item in his appearance is his long hair, which he wears in two plaits down his back. His two braves also wear civilization's garb. But wear heavy boots, into which their trousers are thrust in true western fashion. They speak nothing but their native language.

In 1885 Quanah Parker visited the World's Fair at New Orleans.

The following extract from the Fort Worth *Gazette*, is a recent incident in his career:

"HE BLEW OUT THE GAS"
AND ON THAT BREATH THE SOUL OF YELLOW BEAR
FLEW TO ITS HAPPY HUNTING GROUNDS.

*Another instance in which the noble red man succumbs to the
influence of civilization!*

A sensation was created on the streets yesterday by the news of a tragedy from asphyxiation at the Pickwick hotel, of which two noted Indians, Quanah Parker and Yellow Bear, were the victims.

The circumstances of the unfortunate affair were very difficult to obtain because of the inability of the only two men who were possessed of definite information on the subject to reveal it—one on account of death, and the other from unconsciousness. The Indians arrived here yesterday from the Territory, on the Fort Worth & Denver incoming train. They registered at the Pickwick and were assigned an apartment together in the second story of the building. Very little is known of their subsequent movements, but from the best evidence that can be collected it appears that Yellow Bear retired alone about 10 o'clock, and that in his utter ignorance of modern appliances, he blew out the gas. Parker, it is believed, did not seek his room until 2 or 3 o'clock in the morning, when, not detecting from some cause the presence of gas in the atmosphere, or not locating its origin in the room, he shut the door and scrambled into bed, unmindful of the deadly forces which were even then operating so disastrously.

The failure of the two Indians to appear at breakfast or dinner caused the hotel clerk to send a man around to awake them. He found the door locked and was unable to get a response from the inmates. The room was then forcibly entered, and as the door swung back the rush of the deathly perfume through the aperture told the story. A ghastly spectacle met the eyes of the hotel *employés*. By the bedside in a crouched position, with his face pressed to the floor, was Yellow Bear, in the half-nude condition which Indian fashion in night clothes admits. In the opposite corner near the window, which was closed, Parker was stretched at full length upon his back. Yellow Bear was stone dead, while the quick gasps of his companion indicated that he was in but a stone's throw of eternity. The chief was removed to the bed, and through the untiring efforts of Drs. Beall and Moore his life has been saved.

Finding Quanah sufficiently able to converse, the reporter of the *Gazette* questioned him as to the cause of the unhappy occurrence, and elicited the following facts:

'I came,' said the chief, 'into the room about midnight, and found Yellow Bear in bed. I lit the gas myself. I smelt no gas

QUANAH PARKER.

when I came into the room. When I went to bed I turned the gas off. I did not blow it out. After a while I smelt the gas, but went to sleep. I woke up and shook Yellow Bear and told him 'I'm mighty sick and hurting all over.' Yellow Bear says, 'I'm mighty sick, too.' I got up, and fell down and all around the room, and that's all I know about it.'

'Why didn't you open the door?' asked the reporter.

'I was too crazy to know anything,' replied the chief.

It is indeed, a source of congratulation that the chief will recover, as otherwise his tribe could not be made to understand the occurrence, and results detrimental to those having interests in the Territory would inevitably follow.

The new town of Quanah, in Hardeman county, Texas, was named in honour of chief Quanah Parker.

We will now conclude our little work by appending the following letter, which gives a true pen portrait of the celebrated chief as he appears at his home on the "reservation:"

Anadarko, I. T., Feb. 4, 1886.

We visited Quanah in his *tepee*. He is a fine specimen of physical manhood, tall, muscular—as straight as an arrow; gray, look-you-straight-through-the-eyes, very dark skin, perfect teeth, and a heavy, raven-black hair—the envy of feminine hearts—he wears hanging in two rolls wrapped around with red cloth. His hair is parted in the middle the scalp-lock is a portion of hair the size of a dollar, plaited and tangled, signifying: 'If you want fight you can have it.'

Quanah is how camped with a thousand of his subjects at the foot of some hills near Anadarko. Their white *tepees*, and the inmates dressed in their bright blankets and feathers, cattle grazing, children playing, lent a weird charm to the lonely, desolate hills, lately devastated by prairie fire.

"He has three squaws, his favourite being the daughter of Yellow Bear, who met his death by asphyxiation at Fort Worth in December last. He said he gave seventeen horses for her. His daughter Cynthia, named for her grandmother, Cynthia Parker, is an inmate of the Indian Agent's house. Quanah was at tired in a full suit of buck-skin tunic, leggins and *moccasins* elaborately trimmed in beads—a red breech-cloth, with ornamental ends hanging down. A very handsome and expensive

Mexican blanket was thrown around his body; in his ears were little stuffed birds. His hair done with the feathers of bright plumaged birds. He was handsomer by far than any Ingomar the writer has ever seen—but there was no squaw fair enough to personate his Parthenia. His general aspect, manners, bearing, education, natural intelligence, show plainly that white blood trickles through his veins. When travelling he assumes a complete civilian's outfit—dude collar, watch and chain—takes out his ear-rings—he of course cannot cut off his long hair, saying that he could no longer be 'big chief.' He has a handsome carriage; drives a pair of matched grays, always travelling with one of his squaws (to do the chores). Minna-a-ton-ccha is with him now. She knows no English, but while her lord is conversing, gazes, dumb with admiration, at 'my lord'—ready to obey his slightest wish or command.

JANNETTE E. DE CAMP SWEET

Mrs. J. E. De Camp Sweet's Narrative of Her Captivity in the Sioux Outbreak of 1862

After a lapse of more than thirty years I am solicited to write an account of my captivity among the Sioux Indians during the massacre of 1862. It is a part of my life which I would much rather forget than remember, and which, after so many years' time, I can now dwell upon but with feelings of the utmost horror.

It is not my purpose in these pages to attempt a portrayal of the dreadful scenes enacted on that 18th day of August, 1862, and the many following ones—days so replete with savage atrocity that each moment of time seemed written over in lurid characters of blood and fire. It will only be necessary to dwell upon the subject long enough to record the most important events which history desires to preserve.

Many things have been written concerning the tragedies of that dreadful period; but, as far as I know, none who were eyewitnesses have attempted to narrate what passed in the Indian camp during those dreadful weeks. Having been an actor in the sad drama which desolated and almost depopulated some of the finest portions of our fair state, I will try to give as accurate a description of what I saw and heard during those fateful four weeks which followed the 18th of August as length of time and lapse of memory will permit. Of the brutalities perpetrated during those dreadful days (seemingly multiplied into years, so dreadful now they appear to me), nothing that could be written could describe the actual occurrences which took place from the inception of the massacre to its close.

Then woman's shriek was heard in vain,
Nor infancy's unpitied plain
More than the warrior's groan could gain,
Respite from ruthless butchery.

For more than a year we had lived among them on terms of friendly intimacy, if I may so describe it. They were daily visitors at our home—not always welcome ones, it is true. They came with their bead work, game, fish or anything which they happened to have, to trade for pork, sugar, flour or anything which they needed most, and always expected to receive in return more than twice the value of any article brought. It was not a pleasant life among them, but we tried to make the best of it while we were there. The Indians, with few exceptions, were kind and peaceable, and after a few months I grew so accustomed to their presence that no thought of fear ever entered my mind.

My husband had charge of the mills which sawed the lumber for their houses, and during the autumn following our removal there put in a mill for grinding the corn which the Indians raised on their lands. They came almost daily with their bags of corn to be ground, and would linger about the doors and windows, asking questions and receiving answers about everything usually discussed, and in their childish way comprehending many things; but they seemed more especially interested in the conflict between our disrupted states. Our daily papers came in each weekly budget of mail, and those of us who had friends at the front eagerly scanned the lists for news of our loved ones. Nothing seemed more terrible then than waiting for news from the seat of war.

How well I remember the usual reply when asking my husband for news. "All quiet on the Potomac" was invariably his answer.

Of course the Indians could not help knowing of our many reverses during that and the following year, and drew their own conclusions. Not until I became a captive did I realize how they put things together and which seemed to have woven a web of fate around their unconscious victims. They often described, most accurately, the accounts of the terrible battles in which our defeats were more numerous than our victories and when the call came for additional troops and they were actually enlisted in our very midst, taking half-bloods, employees, every one for soldiers, small wonder that they should think our government in the last throes of dissolution. The winter preceding the massacre set in cold and snowy, the roads were drifted and almost impassable. There was a great amount of suffering among the Indians, as their crops had been bad from drought and cut-worms, and there was much sickness attendant upon starvation, of which there were actual cases.

Mr. De Camp (my husband) gave me leave to feed the women and children who were most destitute, and we otherwise alleviated their distress many times when they would not go to Dr. Humphrey, the government physician. The doctor was not a favourite with them, and they preferred to take the medicines which I often prepared for their little ones. I have related the foregoing only to show that "*the good will of a dog is better than the ill will."* Owing to the deep snow, the roads were almost impassable and government supplies became scanty. The weekly issues of flour, pork, etc., failed to meet the wants of so many hungry people, and at Christmas time things looked very gloomy. We concluded that we must do something for those who most needed help, and accordingly opened the cellar, distributing many bushels of vegetables to those who were actually suffering. I cannot doubt that our friendly attitude toward those starving wretches eventually became the means of our preservation from horrid tortures and a lingering death.

There were many things, of almost daily occurrence which showed that the Indians were very much dissatisfied with their condition, but we gave no heed, supposing it had always been so before, and knowing that there was much jealousy between the various bands, some thinking that others were better treated by the agent than themselves. My husband was made a confidant of many grievances, as he was invariably kind to all. They named him Chan-ba-su-da-su-da-cha, the friendly man. He was always very loyal to the agent also, knowing that he was trying to do all he could for them, and he would tell them to have patience and the government in time would do all it had promised and that the agent was not to blame for the supplies or the weather. June, the month for the annual payment, came and no money came with it. July passed and the Indians grew angry and believed what the traders told them—that "that payment, if ever made, would be the last." I could never understand why the traders should have told such things; but I was assured by many of the wisest among the Indians that it was what the traders told them more than anything else that caused the uprising. How surely they atoned for it with their lives history does not fail to record.

The day preceding the outbreak Mr. De Camp started for St. Paul to transact some business with the agent when he should arrive there. Maj. Galbraith had gone on with the enlisted men, and my husband expected to overtake them at St. Peter, go on to St. Paul and return by Saturday, at the latest, to the agency. Not a dream of danger was in either of our minds, but the separation for even a week seemed long in anticipation. Nothing but the most pressing business, which required his immediate attention, could have induced him to leave me, as our youngest child was ill; but I urged him to go, knowing how necessary it was for him to do so, and pretended to feel much braver than I actually did. Monday morning, after a restless night with my baby, I awoke late, and myself and children (one of whom was nine years and the other four, and the baby) ate our breakfast and afterward I attended to my usual duties. The children went out to play, and the kitchen girls (a half-breed and a German girl) arranged the day's work.

My eldest boy came in and asked me if he might go up to the agency to play with one of his mates. For some reason I told him he could not. We remarked upon the stillness of the morning, in the absence of the noise of the mill and the men being away from work. They had all gone up to the agency, as the mill would not run in Mr. De Camp's absence. About 10 o'clock I went into the garden, and while there I observed an Indian coming out of the stables with the horses harnessed. He immediately hitched them to the wagon and drove along toward the house, my two boys following him. I also observed that he was a stranger, and as he came opposite the door I asked him where he was taking our horses. He replied "that they were his horses and that everything else was his thereabouts. That all the white people had been killed up there," pointing to the agency, "and you had better be getting out of this." All this was said in the Dakota language. He did not offer to stop but drove immediately on toward the ferry.

Lucy, the half-breed, hearing what he said, immediately began to scream that we would all be murdered. I told her I did not believe a word of it, that he had said so just to get the horses, and that if the whites had been killed we would have heard the guns and the shouts. The German girl hurriedly bundled up her clothes and started with all speed to the ferry, about a quarter of a mile above us, and I never saw her again. Lucy, the half-breed, urged me to fly, as she was sure it was all true; so, taking my sick boy out of his cradle, we started for the top of the hill.

As soon as we arrived there I saw it was all too true. The agency buildings and the traders' stores were in flames and hundreds of shouting savages were surging about the government warehouse, shrieking and brandishing their weapons. Paralyzed with fear, I knew not where to turn. I looked toward the ferry and I saw a dense crowd surrounding it. I knew that all hope was cut off in that quarter. It seemed incredible that all this had gone on without our knowledge, that not a sound had penetrated to our place where all had been so still! I could not reason, much less hope, that we could escape; but while I stood there motionless (Lucy having fled at the first sight), an old squaw, Chief Wacouta's mother, came running past. As she came up she cried, "*Puck-a-chee! Puck-a-chee! Dakota, mepo-wa-sicha squaw! Puck-a-chee!*" "Fly! fly! they will kill you, white squaw!" and she threw my four-year-old boy over her shoulder, not stopping a moment.

I followed with the other children, running toward Wabasha's village, about a mile away. Just before we reached it we met a large body of Indians in war paint, armed with guns and bows and arrows. Each had a war club and tomahawk and were brandishing them in an excited manner. Chief Wabasha was sitting on a large white horse, looking as if just out of one of Catlin's pictures. He was dressed in chief's costume, a head-dress of red flannel adorned with bullock horns and eagle feathers, wings of feathers over his shoulders and down his back, great strings of beads around his neck and a belt of *wampum* around his waist. His lower limbs were clad in fringed buckskin and he carried a beautiful rifle across his lap, with two pistols in their holsters. He had no other arms.

Every detail seemed to strike me as if photographed. I can yet see him, sitting like a Centaur, haranguing his men, and, as he rode up, he dismounted. Drawing his pistols from their holsters he approached us. I felt that our time had come to die. I immediately fell on my knees, imploring him to spare our lives and asking him to remember what we had done for his sick child the past winter. The Indians, sullen and scowling, crowded around closer and closer, raising their tomahawks as if ready to strike, when Wabasha thrust them back, and, presenting his pistols, told them that I should not be killed. He said that I was a good squaw, and called them cowards and squaws for wanting to kill women and children. They were very angry and determined; but, after a long speech, in which he told them that he would not be accessory to what had been done and that he should protect and defend the whites as long as he could, they mounted their ponies and rode off. Wacouta's mother had disappeared, and Wabasha, seeing we were still so much frightened, told us to follow him.

We entered a house near, in which he said we would be safe, as all the Indians had gone to the agency, and he would ride up and see what had been done. He told us it was the upper Indians who were doing all the mischief, and that he would always be a friend of the whites, and would see that we were not killed. He then rode away. (It was nearly two weeks before I saw him again, when he came to bid me goodbye before he started with the Indian soldiers on an expedition somewhere below.) After he was gone the children became so frightened, fearing others would come, that we left the building and wandered toward the river, hoping we might find some way of crossing. But finding none we sat down in a clump of bushes, not daring to go out on the open prairie lest we should meet Indians.

All this time I felt assured that it was the Sissetons, as Wabasha had said, who were doing the killing, as I had not yet recognized any whom I knew of the lower bands among those with Wabasha. We remained hidden in the bushes by the river until the sun was setting, when I saw an Indian, whom I recognized, coming down the bluff toward a house nearby. It proved to be one who had often been to our house asking favours and to whom we had sent a man to help him put up a stove but a short while before. Feeling sure he would aid me, I made myself known, telling him how hungry the children were, and asking what had happened. He said that all the whites who had not escaped from the agency had been killed, but did not say by whom. I asked if he had seen Wabasha. He said there had been a battle and he might have been among the killed, but did not tell me that it was with the white soldiers they had fought. He said the lower bands were in camp just below the agency and he was going back there. I asked him if he would protect us into camp. He said he would do all he could, but feared the warriors would kill us.

Still thinking that the lower bands were friendly to us and that they were arrayed against the Sissetons, I told him we would go with him, as we could not stay there. We went with him to camp, which we reached just at dark. Instead of meeting friends, as I supposed we would, there were only angry, sullen faces on all sides. Everywhere were piles of goods from the stores and houses, and they were angrily discussing the ownership among themselves. I then knew that those whom we had relied on as friends were our enemies. I asked a squaw for some food for the children, but she did not pretend to hear me. Seeing an Indian leading one of our horses by the bridle, I went to him and asked him if he would not help us and give us some food. I knew him well and had often fed his family, but he said he did not know anything about us and we had better be getting out of the camp or we would be killed.

I asked him if he knew of any place where we could go and be safe. He replied: "You can swim the river. It is better to drown than be *tomahawked*." I looked in vain among all that excited assemblage to find one friendly face upon whom I could rely in my present extremity. The instinct of the savage had been fully aroused and blood and plunder was their only desire. Feeling sure that we would receive scant mercy if we remained where we were, I determined to creep silently out and hide in the grass till they should remove from there, or perhaps get far enough away to escape them altogether. I had scarcely resolved to do so when I saw Wacouta (the chief who had lived nearest us) approaching as if he were seeking someone. I went immediately to him and asked his protection. He said, "Come with me. You are in danger here," and lifting my little boy in his arms he rapidly led the way out of camp.

We followed and soon came to one of his empty houses. He opened the door, and, bidding us go inside, he gave me a small box of figs and left, locking the door on the outside. Feeling momentarily secure, I tried to hush the frightened children, giving them the figs to eat, as they had had no food since morning. They then knelt down and said their evening prayer, and, drawing close to me in the darkness, were soon sleeping the innocent sleep of childhood. What words could convey the feeling of complete desolation which seized me as I sat there dwelling on the events of the past day and the prospects of the coming morrow? Twice we had been rescued; but would Wacouta do as he had said? Would he be able to protect us from their hellish deeds? I did not fear death so much for myself, but the thought of seeing my children perish before my eyes, or leaving them to be the victims of a cruelty surpassing death, I felt that I could not endure it! Wacouta had assured me on the way that he was a true friend of the whites and would save as many as he could. But I knew that the warriors would not be controlled by their chiefs, and that nothing would stay their murderous hands when once aroused.

Besides all else, they had found plenty of liquor on the reservation, and a drunken Indian was more to be dreaded than a tiger in the jungle. While thinking this I was alarmed to hear someone trying to unfasten the door, and, hearing voices, I discerned that of Mattie Williams. They unfastened the door, and, entering, I was surprised to see both Miss Williams and Mary Anderson with two Indians. They had just been brought there in a wagon and Mary at once hastened to tell me that she had been shot in the back. She was in great pain and apprehensive of immediate death. The three girls, Miss Williams, a niece of J. B. Reynolds, who had come out on a visit from Painesville, Ohio, and was expecting to return in a few days, and Mary Anderson and Mary Swandt, who were domestics in the family of Mr. Reynolds, upon hearing of the trouble, had started from his place in a wagon in which were Mr. Patoile and Lee Davis of Shakopee.

Mr. and Mrs. Reynolds were in a buggy and they all started together. After a short time they became separated. Those in the wagon were near the fort, on the opposite side of the river, when they were overtaken. The men were killed and the girls ran away, but were soon overtaken, Mary Anderson being shot in the back, the ball lodging in the abdomen. They were brought into camp after dark and were brought where I then was. In a few moments the negro, Godfrey, came in with Mary Swandt, and then a crowd of Indians, armed with guns and carrying the knapsacks of the soldiers killed that day at the ferry. In a moment all was terror and confusion.

Lights were struck, curses and imprecations resounded on all sides. The children, by this time awakened, were terror stricken. Mary Anderson was urging Mattie and myself to extract the bullet from her body, thinking it would save her. Mary Swandt had fled to me for protection from their indecent assaults, begging me to tell her what they said. My eldest boy was crying, "Are we going to be killed now, mamma? Don't let them kill us with knives!" Nothing could describe that awful scene.

It was as if the fiends that fell
Had pealed the banner cry of hell.

Shocked into a feeling of desperation and an absence of fear, I determined to tell them how it would end, even if they killed me while doing it. Some of the young men I knew. They had often come to me to learn English words. Turning to them I asked what had instigated them to do the deeds they had done. They replied that it was such fun to kill white men. They were such cowards that they all ran away and left their squaws to be killed, and that one Indian could kill ten white men without trying. Without fear, I told them that they would all be hanged before another moon; that if the white men had gone away they would soon return; that "the whispering spirit" (the telegraph) would at once bring more men than would cover the prairies, and that if they did kill us it would not be long till their hideous forms would be dangling from a rope's end. How they scoffed and jeered as they swung their rifles and *tomahawks* around their heads, aiming to strike as near as they could without hitting.

The fiendish work went on until the uproar became so loud and furious that Wacouta appeared, having heard the din and the shooting. Going up to his two sons, who were among the crowd (boys not more than sixteen), he demanded of them how they came there and what they were doing. Then, thrusting them out of the door, he cleared the rest, who seemed to have nearly all been of his band. The most of them were so drunk they could hardly stand. Turning to me, he asked how long this had been going on, and I told him everything that had been done while he was away. He seemed distressed beyond measure to know that his sons had been of the number. Telling us not to fear further molestation, he turned to Mary and asked what he could do for her. She told him to try to take the bullet out of her body, and, using an old jack knife, he probed the wound, first taking out the pieces of wadding and finally found the ball quite near the surface. He brought some water, and, tearing up an old apron, soaked it and placed it on the wound.

The poor girl had grown delirious, and we all knew that the wound was fatal. Gathering some old clothes together for her to lie on, we lifted her on a rude bedstead, and Wacouta left us, telling us that he would keep watch that we should not be disturbed again. The terrors and fatigues of the past day were succeeded by broken slumbers, from which we would arouse at the slightest noise, and I will say in passing that I do not think I had one hour's real sleep in the four weeks I was a captive. Morning dawned at last, and Wacouta came according to promise, telling us that we must stay there as the Indians were preparing to go below to attack Fort Ridgely. He said we must not show ourselves outside until he returned. I asked in surprise if he were going and he said yes! That his band would kill him if he did not He carried Mary up the stairs to the loft, told us to follow, and, bringing us a pail of water, shut the trap door of our prison and left us again, impressing upon us the necessity of remaining perfectly quiet.

No food was left us to eat, to which I called Wacouta's attention; but he said there was no time then to get any, as his band was waiting for him and he must be off. We could see from a hole in the chamber the gay cavalcade marching by. The bodies of the warriors were entirely destitute of clothing except the loin cloth, which they invariably wore, and a blanket worn loosely round the neck, floating to the breeze as their ponies pranced and cavorted. They were painted in all the colours of the rainbow, and their ponies were decked with ribbons and tassels of every bright hue. The chiefs were dressed in their war costume, which I have before described. They rode gaily away, shouting and whooping as only an Indian can.

We now turned our attention to our own situation. Mary was in a violent delirium of fever, calling for food, and there was not a morsel to give her. My baby lay perfectly passive, and did not seem to notice anything. How long we were to remain there depended alone on the Indians' return, and the families of the Indians had left the camp for the upper villages when the warriors started below. Unless the whites came to rescue us (which we dared not hope for after the battle at the ferry became known to us) we might starve before help came, and but for Wacouta's strict injunctions a part of us would have gone in search of food. We could see the scouts riding past from our post of observation and knew that they were watching.

Mary became so violent in her ravings that we feared discovery, and Wednesday night Mattie and Mary Swandt went out in the darkness and found some green corn in a field not far away. Bringing it in, we ate ravenously of the raw corn and tried to give Mary some. But she would not eat it, crying all the time that "we wanted, to starve her! and if only Dr. Daniels would come he would cure her!" Thursday, about noon, the war party returned, some of them passing the house we were in. At last a wagon stopped and took Mary Swandt away. Then another, which took Mattie Williams, and at last a man, whom I knew, drove up and told us to get ready and go with him to the camp above. I got into the wagon with my baby in my arms; then he lifted Mary and placed her head in my lap and the two children crept into the bottom of the wagon at our feet. Mary's limbs were getting rigid and she could scarcely speak; but I hoped she would live until we reached the camp.

Our way lay through the streets of the agency, where the bodies of the first day's victims were still lying. It was an awful sight, and I tried to screen the children from seeing the dead. When we came to where the stores had been I saw Divoll, one of Myrick's clerks, lying extended on the burnt floor, his features looking natural as in life but the body burnt to a cinder. Myrick, Lynde and others lay there outside. Some of them had been decapitated, but the Indians did not touch them then or seem to notice them. Just as we were passing the last building which, for some cause, had not been fired, they began to stone the windows and set fire to them.

A dreadful storm had been gathering for some time, and just as the buildings were fired it burst with great fury upon us. The noise of the thunder and the flashing of the lightning, together with the roaring and crackling of the flames from the burning houses, made a scene not easily forgotten, and the horrors of that ride will never be effaced. The cavalcade numbered many hundreds and seemed one sad, unending caravan. No pen could describe the hideous features of those painted demons as they rode frantically backward and forward outside the wagons, yelling and shouting and brandishing their weapons with their hands still reeking with the murders they had committed.

I will not dwell longer upon it, but say that we at last came to Little Crow's village, where a part of the Indians had camped, and there we found Mattie, who had just arrived. The Indian who claimed the dying Mary came up and said she must get out there. I told him she was dying and to let her go on with me so that I could be with her till the last. He brutally said, "She is better than two dead squaws yet. Get along out!"

Mattie came up and we lifted her out and they carried her into a tent as I left, Mattie promising to bury her. She lived about an hour after, reviving, however, to take a little food which Mattie gave her. She was buried there with an old tablecloth wrapping her and in the autumn her friends removed her. We went on farther to Shakopee village, near where Redwood now stands, and remained there until the next Monday, when the whole of the bands went up near Rice Creek, where they camped until after the battle of Birch Coulie. The morning after our arrival at Shakopee camp the Indians were alert very early, having made preparations for attacking the fort. They had prepared arrows with combustible material in order to shoot into the roofs of the buildings to burn them. They were very sanguine of success that day, and rode away saying that they would not come back before "*Esan-tanka-tupee*" (meaning the "big knife fort") was taken.

How they gloated over the anticipated spoils of the day and talked of the good things in the "commissary" and the number of guns and the ammunition, and, above all, the pleasure of hewing down and scalping their enemies! Glad as we were to see them ride away, our anxiety was greater, fearing they would succeed. During the afternoon an old squaw mounted one of the lookouts which belong to every village and called my attention to a vast volume of smoke rising far off on the prairie in the direction of the fort. She seemed frenzied with joy, saying to me, "Look! look! see the big steamboat coming! Hurry and get ready to go."

My heart died within me as I saw the flames and smoke mount higher and higher and thought of what might be taking place in the doomed garrison. The squaws made haste to leave with their ponies and wagons, if they were fortunate enough to have them, to be in at the plundering of the fort. I had just had an interview with Frank Roy, a half-breed, and he said that he feared they would succeed. If they did not, that himself, John Moore and some others had determined to get us away if possible. Saturday the Indians began to return in straggling parties, bringing large quantities of goods of every description. Some had been to New Ulm, and the harrowing tales they told of murder and destruction nearly froze our blood. Godfrey told of killing seventeen women and children and would relate how they fought for their lives before they were killed. Sunday the warriors returned and were feasted according to their custom.

That day a woman was shot in our camp for trying to escape. Monday morning the tents were taken down and orders were given to march. The whole of the lower bands were in motion early in the day, and the cavalcade started. Their haste was so great that we were sure the white troops were after them. When we came to Redwood river crossing the stream was greatly swollen from recent rains and all on foot were compelled to wade. In the rush of teams I felt sure we would be crushed, but I hastily threw my four-year-old boy on to a wagon, the other climbing up behind him, and with my baby in my arms I addressed myself to the river, plunging bravely through in order to keep near my other children. I never knew how I got over; but when on the other side I missed my shoes, which I had taken off in order to have them dry when I landed, and was compelled to go on without them.

The Indian in whose tent I had been was wounded at New Ulm and had to be carried in a litter, and we had strict orders to keep close to the litter at all times and not get away from our friends. As we reached the place where Mr. Reynolds had lived the train halted for fresh water from the spring. When our turn came and I was raising the water to my lips I heard a shout, and looking up saw a horrible form bending over me just ready to strike. It was "Cut Nose," who had sworn to kill every man, woman and child that he was able to kill. I darted quickly round behind the litter containing my friend, whose voice had saved my life, and after that experience was careful to keep as close to our party as possible.

I wish it were possible for me to describe that march upward. Long lines of wagons, carriages, ponies with poles trailing (as customary with the Indians); each vehicle loaded to its utmost capacity, without regard to size or capability (many of which would suddenly collapse, leaving the occupant stranded, as it were, in mid ocean). The long lines of cattle driven before each band, and the horses lashed without mercy, the warriors riding outside of the cavalcade in order to prevent any escaping, all combined to render it a scene which, once looked upon, could never be forgotten. There were numberless flags carried in the procession. Two or three were of the largest size, but where procured I never knew. One of Wabasha's band, "Old Brave," had one which he said was given him in Washington once when he went there with other Indians years before.

The negro Godfrey is one who always stands out most prominently in my memory, not excepting "Cut Nose." He was everywhere; up and down the line he rode, passing us twenty times an hour and always trying to frighten the captives by his hideous antics. Many of the warriors wore ladies' bonnets on their heads, and furs dragged downward from their legs. Their breasts were covered with brooches and chains of value; from their ears depended wheels from clocks and watches which they had destroyed. The finest silks were made into shirts; beautiful shawls were used for saddle cloths and cut up for head-dresses and waist girdles. There was no device too ridiculous for their attire and nothing too costly for them to destroy. How often I wished that I might have some of my own comfortable garments to keep us from the cold, but no amount of asking would induce them to give us so much as a blanket, and as the nights were cold, although the days were hot, we needed covering, especially as our bed was the bare earth, often soaked with rain.

How vividly I remember the time when a medicine man came to doctor my wounded friend, who was about to die. We were all thrust out of the tent and sat huddled together for warmth till nearly midnight, when the evil spirit, having been ejected from the sick man and shot at as it departed, we were allowed to return. While we were sitting outside an old squaw named Hazatome came along, and seeing us huddled together began to exclaim at our poverty. She had often came to our house and been kindly used. Her pity was so great that she offered to give each of us an Indian costume. Never doubting her sincerity, I was greatly pleased and told her I would come for it the next day.

I ran the risk of going some distance from our lodge to meet her and receive the clothing. Some fresh scalps had just been brought in and the Indians were having a dance, so I thought I need not fear. I found Hazatome and asked her for the articles, fully persuaded that they would be forthcoming. Imagine my surprise when she would not utter a word. She neither affirmed nor denied having promised them, but simply ignored me altogether. I could not help crying with disappointment, but left her, thinking I would never believe or trust an Indian again. On our way up we came upon the body of George Gleason, who had been killed on the 18th as he was coming down from Yellow Medicine. I had known him before coining to the reservation. All that day we were hoping that the whites would come, as the Indians seemed in great haste, urging on the captives with frequent threats if they did not hurry faster.

My elder boy would carry the younger one on his back until exhausted, and then I would carry both him and the baby together. In contrast to what I have related of Indian character I will relate here a little incident of that day's journey. We had stopped to rest for a few moments, something having happened to the train, when I saw an old man, who had been a constant visitor at our house during the winter. I had felt great pity for him, as he was very old and feeble, and he said his wife was ill. He came three times a week to get his dinner, and I always sent food to his wife. He seemed very much surprised to see me and the children, asked where Chan-ba-su-da-su-da-cha was; if he had been massacred, etc, and darting away, came back leading an old squaw to where we were standing. He was telling her who we were and how good we had been to them, saying that then I had everything and now I was a poor captive, without food or clothes.

The old man's eloquence touched me deeply as I contrasted my situation with what it had been, and we were all bathed in tears. He brought up his pony, with poles fastened behind, and reaching a bundle brought out some pieces of bread and gave to the children, who were almost famished. He then fixed the bundles so that my little boy could ride, but no persuasion on our parts could induce him to leave me a moment. The poor old man had tried to comfort us the best he could, and I did not soon forget his attempted kindness in my forlorn state. The following morning we were roused early and the camp was soon in motion. The Indians were constantly on the lookout as they feared pursuit. That day we reached Rice Creek, having made a wide detour from the main road; consequently we travelled much farther than if we had gone direct. Here they stayed several days. The encampment was very large, about one thousand tents, I should think. It was like a city. The tents were upon the outside, facing inward, and the cattle and horses and wagons were in the centre.

There I first saw Mrs. Hunter, whose husband had been killed near the fort, and many other captives. Mrs. Hunter was in John Moore's tent, and I think Mrs. A. Robertson and her son Frank. We were not far apart, and Mattie and myself often visited Mrs. Hunter, and we read the *Litany* in the prayer book together, as Mrs. Hunter was the only one who had one. Mr. Moore was very kind to us, and said he wanted very much to help us get away to the fort. While we were at Rice Creek they held a council, erecting a large tent and displaying the United States flag from the centre. Frank Roy, a half-breed, and John Moore felt certain that we would be sent to Fort Ridgely, but after the council was ended told us not to go if they did send us, for some of the parties who advocated our going meant to lie in wait and murder us on the way.

It was while here I first learned that my husband was living and that he was at Fort Ridgely. Some messengers had been sent down to see what the whites were going to do about the captives and when they returned told us that the agent, Dr. Wakefield, Mr. De Camp and others were there. From that moment I resolved that I would escape in some manner. Scouting parties were out the most of the time, and it was here I first met Wabasha after his leaving us on the first day. A large war party were assembling to go below, and Wabasha came to shake hands and bid me goodbye. I was surprised to see him and asked him where he was going. He pointed to his face, which was painted black with white lines running through it. I asked him if he were going to kill his white brothers and told him that I thought he was a friend of the whites. He said he was obliged to go, but that he would not kill any one he "would shoot up." I told him how sorry I was to see him go to war, but he only said, "I shake hands," meaning goodbye, and was gone.

This was the party we afterwards learned that fought at Birch Coulie. In a short time we were again on the march and camped above the upper agency next time. The second or third day after the war party left, runners came into camp in great haste and ordered the squaws to run bullets as fast as they could, and all was consternation and uproar. I could not find out what had happened, but knew afterward that there had been a battle. I here met Lucy for the first time. She had heard that I was somewhere in camp and sought me out. I told her that I intended to try to escape; that we were almost starving and we might as well end the matter at once. She said that if I dare try she would help me that night to go to her uncle's, an upper Indian, and I

66

could there get more to eat. In the confusion of the camp we could easily slip away, as all the warriors had gone and only a few old men remained in camp.

We had three miles to go that night, and I found I was growing very weak. Lucy carried the baby a while and then the other one, as we were in great haste to get there. That night I found real friends. The grandmother (Lorenzo's mother) was one of Dr. Williamson's first converts to Christianity. Having been a renowned medicine woman, she had great influence among the bands and she was a very superior squaw. She and her daughter cooked a nice supper of beef and bread and placed it on the table, and we ate with such appetites as hunger alone can give. It was the first real food in many weeks. That night we rested quietly away from the pandemonium of the camp. In the morning someone brought the news that the Indians would move up to Dr. Riggs' mission at once, and as soon as we could eat our breakfast we started on foot to get there before them.

I knew that I would be safer there, as there were many Christian Indians there. John Renville was in charge after the escape of Dr. Riggs' and Dr. Williamson's families. The Indians had sent them word that they were coming to burn the mission and wanted them all to put on Indian dress and go into tents. Paul Lorenzo and Simon were elders in Dr. Riggs' church and they at once took 'down the bell and buried it, and taking the books from the library, scooped out a large hole, and, lining it with blankets, placed them in it and covered it up carefully. The Indians came on Thursday afternoon and began to burn the buildings, the other Indians having gone into tents. They encamped on the other side of a small *coulie*, as they said they could kill the Christians better if they were by themselves. It was another dreadful time for us all, and I had given up all hope of our friends ever coming. We knew there had been a battle, but could learn nothing about it, only they claimed they had killed all the whites.

On Saturday a large party returned from somewhere and Sunday the rest came in, bringing more captives. All this time I had kept hidden from them, and I afterward learned that they were out hunting for us. Late Sunday evening, Lorenzo, the son of the medicine woman, returned with his mother to camp from which they had started in the early part of the day, bringing in some large turtles which they proceeded to dress for the evening meal. Not a word was said by any one until after we had eaten and the children were asleep. The messengers of Little Crow had returned from the fort, telling him that Gen. Sibley would not treat with them until they delivered the captives, and he said: "Let them come; we will put the captives before the guns, then he can shoot."

67

An old man went round that evening crying the news and saying that all must be ready to start for Red River in the morning, and all the captives who could not walk would be killed. I knew then that the time had come to try to escape. Lorenzo and Simon sat smoking by the fire in the tent, but neither said a word. I felt sure they meant to try to help us escape, but Lorenzo's wife did not want to leave her people, and she was much afraid of the whites. I knew that we could never walk to British America, that we were even then unable to walk any distance, and that it would only end our troubles the sooner if we were killed while trying to escape.

About 3 o'clock in the morning Lorenzo's mother came to us and said: "If you want to get away, now is the time." I arose very quickly, and, gathering my children together, found Lorenzo and his family ready to start. We crept out of the tent on our hands and knees, I with my baby clasped close to my breast. The children showed remarkable presence of mind, and no noise was made in any way. I expected every moment to hear the shot fired that would end our lives, but I knew that death was behind if we stayed. We reached the *chaparral* without being discovered, and there we met the mother of Lorenzo with a few handfuls of flour tied up in a rag for our provision on the way. She said it was all she could give us and seemed greatly troubled lest we should be missed and a search made for us. But Lorenzo knew that in the hurry of their departure they would scarcely miss us, there would be so much confusion.

The old squaw seemed much affected at parting with her son, but refused all his entreaties to go with us, saying "she was an aged tree and the branches were all cut off," and that she would die among her people. She embraced us all, and, commending us to the care of Him whom she tried to serve, left us and returned to camp. Lorenzo led the way toward the river, and we walked in Indian file, he returning every little way to cover up our tracks and straighten the vines which covered the ground. He would not allow us to step on a log, but step carefully over, and in this way we reached a marshy lake, which we entered, wading in some distance, where he broke down the tall reeds growing there and made a place for us to sit, although in the water. It was just dawn when we entered the marsh.

In a short time we heard the camp astir, with its usual noise, and we fully expected pursuit. Soon the usual sounds of breaking camp were heard. Guns were fired, drums beaten, dogs barked and unearthly shoutings filled the air. Being on lower ground the noises seemed close at hand. After they had started upward Lorenzo said he must go back to the camp to see if anything had been left that we might need and find out if they had missed us. The squaw (his wife) seemed terribly frightened at his determination, and we all tried to urge him not to do so. But he said he would come back safe, and started off. He said that he crept Indian fashion, with grass and weeds bound about him, until he got safely where they had been. He found a warning left for himself and Simon, saying they, would shoot as many holes in them when found as they had shot into their tents which were left standing. He found two chickens in the bushes, which he killed and brought back with him.

Just at dark he came in unobserved by us till in our midst, when he told the day's story and said we would go out of the lake on to higher ground and wait till morning to go to the river. I urged him to go on that night, but he would not. We were almost famished for water, as the place where we were, although filled with water, was unfit to drink. He would not go, however, and we waded out to dryer ground, where we lay down in the tall grass in which the mosquitoes were so thick that we breathed them with every inhalation. But we were free, and, if wet, hungry and cold and naked, we had escaped from our dreadful captors. Just as day was dawning, we arose and started for the river, where the Indian and his mother had hidden the boats the Sunday before.

When we got to the river we were so overjoyed that we could not wait, but rushed into it, drinking to our hearts' content. My baby, who had seemed in a stupor for so many days, now grew more like himself and said he was hungry. The squaw made preparations for cooking the flour and chickens, but the Indian said she must not, as the smoke would show where we were. Hunger at last prevailed, and he said she might make the bread while he built the fire. We were surrounded by thick woods, and there was little danger of our being detected. It seemed a meal fit for a king so hungry were we; the only trouble was there was not enough of it. We lay hidden all that day, and when night came we embarked in our frail boats. Mine was an Indian dugout but very leaky. We gathered boughs and leaves to put in the bottom and the Indian gave me a cup to bail it out. There was no paddle, only a piece of split board, which was whittled so that I could grasp it. The Indians had taken a great deal of pains to break up and destroy every boat on the river so that the whites could not escape.

The Indian's boat was a skiff with oars. He took his family and my eldest boy with him and I put my four-year-old boy behind me in the boat and carried the baby in my lap. We intended travelling only at night, but found that we could not get over the rapids, as it was dark and raining nearly all the way. The rain began just as we came where the Yellow Medicine empties into the Minnesota, and there I lost my paddle, which made the Indian very angry. The current was so swift, and I was unaccustomed to managing a boat, so I went drifting round and round, expecting every moment to be upset, till he rowed back and gave me one of his. I did not mind his anger so long as we were not drowned. The rain came on so heavily that we could not proceed, and at last got out of our boats, and, climbing up the river bank, laid down in the rain to await another day.

While we were preparing to get into our boats the next morning the Indian saw across the river on the prairie a woman with five children running as fast as she could. He immediately got into the boat and crossed over and in about an hour he brought her and the children to where we were. She had run away in the night and had secreted a few handfuls of crusts, which she had done up in a handkerchief. We had yet a little bread, which the squaw had saved, and that was all our provisions for the journey to the fort. The Indian said he had seen a canoe when we passed down in the night and he went back and brought it for the woman and her children. She was a Mrs. Robideaux, whose husband was an enlisted soldier at the fort (Renville Rangers, Company I, Tenth Minnesota).

The rain did not cease, but we started on. How vigorously I plied the paddle when I knew each stroke brought me nearer liberty and friends! Hunger, fatigue and pain were alike forgotten, or only remembered, as I thought of the possibilities lying before me.

On the afternoon of Thursday we came to a crossing where we thought to remain all night. Suddenly we heard the distant sound of a cow bell; the Indian was alert in an instant. Grasping his gun, he ran into the woods in the direction of the sound and soon we heard one shot and then another, until we counted nine shots. Thinking he had met Indians and was being fired upon, we hid ourselves as quickly as we could and waited. He finally came in with a huge piece of meat over his shoulder which he had cut from the cow he had killed without waiting to skin her. I leave any one to judge how that beef tasted to us after our long fast, as we ate it scarcely waiting for it to be cooked by holding it on sticks close to the blaze.

After a hearty meal we laid down for the night and felt so thankful that it did not rain. The next day we made fires and cut and jerked portions of the beef for the rest of our journey. Late in the afternoon we again started, putting the meat into a separate canoe which the Indian had picked up the day before and in which he put my eldest boy and his own boy, who could paddle the boat. We then had four boats and meat enough to last the journey.

About 9 o'clock in the evening it began to rain, and as we were nearing the site of the agency the Indian had told us to be very quiet, as he feared there might be Indians around. We had heard the barking of dogs and other signs of Indians. We were going along very silently when I heard a splash and gurgle behind me and knew something had happened to the boys' boat. The Indian had taken the lead, the woman and her children next, then my boat and the others came after. I knew that the boat holding the boys was overturned, and that my boy could not swim. At once I shouted to the Indian, who was considerably in advance, that my boy was drowning.

I gave no thought to Indians and our safety, but continued to shout until he came back and began to hunt for the boy. We found his son sitting far out on the roots of the tree that had upset the boat, but he did not utter a sound. When asked where the boat sank he would not reply. It was very dark and raining awfully, but in the continued search the squaw caught my son by the hair as he came to the surface. It seemed an age that he had been in the water and he was unconscious, but we landed at once and succeeded in restoring him. Again we were without food; but that seemed the least of our evils when I thought of the past night's experience. We tried to sleep, but everyone was too excited, the Indian fearing we would be attacked before morning.

We started as usual in the early morning, and about 9 o'clock reached the place where the ferry had been opposite the agency. Seeing the mill and the house still standing I told the Indian that I meant to stop and see if I could recover anything. I knew where my husband kept his papers, and knew also that they would probably not be destroyed unless the house was burned. Feeling something would be needed in setting up business, I resolved to stop. The Indian was very angry, and said everything he could to hinder me. But I was obdurate, and for once had my own way. Seeing that I was determined he also landed and all went up to the house which I had once called home. It was a sad sight which was there presented.

Everything which could not be taken away was torn up and thrown about, feather beds emptied, furniture hacked to pieces and otherwise destroyed. But I found the books and accounts which I was after, and, taking an old satchel, I packed them in it, together with a Bible, which I greatly prized, and we quickly returned to the boats. This visit proved most advantageous to the settlement of my business matters, and the Bible I still keep as a treasured memento of past happy days, the only article which remains to me of all my former possessions.

We passed what we thought the body of Capt. Marsh a short distance below the mill, lying in an eddy among the brush wood, and paddled hastily on, still fearing we would be overtaken. The tortuous river seemed endless, and I often begged the Indian to leave the boats and go on foot the rest of the way. But he would grow angry whenever we broached the subject, always telling how much he had done for us and ending by saying that now, when we were so near our liberties we did not care for his safety. We did not realize, as he did, the danger to which he would be exposed from our troops had we gone in unannounced, for we all looked more or less like aboriginals.

The days went by, however, until Sunday evening came, when suddenly there broke upon our ears a bugle note, followed by the quick tattoo of drums, which told us our long journey was nearly ended and we would again be among friends. From that moment I felt assured of our safety, a feeling to which I had been a stranger for so many dreadful days it seemed that I could not compute them. As we turned a bend in the river the Indian espied a wild goose, which he shot, and we landed. How I besought him to go on! The rain had commenced falling heavily and how could we endure another night lying on the wet ground with our friends so near? But the indomitable will of the Indian prevailed, and we were treated to another lecture on ingratitude, which I made haste to deny, and submitted as cheerfully as possible to the inevitable.

The storm raged furiously all that night, which seemed almost an eternity to me, waiting for I knew not what. Hope and fear alternately seized me. Would I find my husband and we be once more united? Or would my children, whom I had brought so far and through such terrible dangers, be fatherless? The storm at last drove the Indian to our boats, which nearly capsized with the wind and rain, and when we reached the ferry he landed. Leaving his wife and the French woman with their children in the boats, he took my little boy in his arms and we started for the fort. It was situated on a hill some distance from the river, and the rain was running in torrents down the hill. I felt that I could never reach the top so exhausted had I become. My clothing was in rags, an old piece of gingham enveloped my head; my feet were bare and bleeding, as were my children's; but, oh, joy! we were at last free!

Reaching the top of the hill I saw a gentleman come out of the garrison toward us, who proved to be Rev. Joshua Sweet, the chaplain of the post. He advanced to meet us. I asked him if my husband were there. Tears choked his utterance as he said: "I buried him ten days ago." No words can describe the awful desolation of that hour. Every hope seemed blotted out from the horizon of my existence, and life and liberty bought at such a price seemed worthless as I looked at the future of my fatherless children, without a home and many hundred miles from my people. Everyone in the garrison showed us the greatest kindness and means were speedily raised and given me to go to my friends. An escort was also provided to take us to St. Peter, Lieut. Sheehan commanding. It is needless to state that his gentlemanly kindness to us was most gratefully received, as well as that of the other officers who were of the escort, but whose names I do not now remember.

From St. Peter I was sent in the stagecoach to Shakopee, where we had formerly lived and where we were welcomed back as if raised from the dead, so great was the enthusiasm of our reception. Homes were offered by generous friends, clothing was prepared for us, and in a short time my father, an old man of seventy, came as fast as steam could bring him to take me to his Southern home. There, amid the conflict and din of battle, my mother had been laid to rest just one month before the death of my husband. In a few weeks after our arrival I again became a mother, my family now numbering four sons, and we remained in the South until after the war was over and peace restored to the nation as well as families and friends of whom mine were about equally divided.

In 1866 I again returned to Fort Ridgley as the wife of Rev. J. Sweet, the chaplain of the garrison.

I have omitted many things which would be of interest to the reader, and one which I cannot let go unmentioned. Of the many heroic deeds which history has recorded there is one which should be preserved and told to children and their children's children for generations. It is of the heroic ferryman, Manley, who refused time after time to escape, saying "that as long as he knew there was one white person to be ferried over the river, so long would he be there to cross them over." Every heart thrills at deeds of valour done, and every schoolboy has read of Leonidas and his brave men at the pass of Thermopylae who said to his men "*that they were a small number to fight, but enough to die.*"

But Manley knew that he alone must endure the rage of those infuriated savages. His name should be inscribed among those whom their country delights to honour, for, though an obscure man, he was a hero of the grandest type amidst the many heroes of that dreadful time. Time would almost fail to record the deeds of heroism and bravery of both men and women during the period of which I am writing. In the tent, on the battlefield, at home praying for the loved ones, five awful years were passing, years which now recorded seem like a passing tale, but to the participants so awfully real that memory cannot even now dwell upon them without a pity so vast as to be unexplainable.

This narrative would not be complete without an account of the participation of my husband in the battle of Birch Coulie, where he fell mortally wounded. Being almost distracted in mind at the probable fate of his family, he and others used every exertion to prevail on the commander to send out a party to bury the dead or seek the living. Accordingly, he with others started on that ill-fated expedition from which he was destined to return with no knowledge of his loved ones and only death awaiting him. Of his bravery he gave ample proof, as is recorded by those who were with him and saw him shot down. Maj. Galbraith told me the story afterward, how his old Sharp's rifle did rapid work as soon as they were attacked, and that while he was standing at his side holding up something to shield my husband from the enemy's firing he saw an Indian aim directly at him. He fell down and evaded the bullet, rising again to shoot before the other could load, but the Indian had a double-barrel and shot just as he raised up, the ball entering his head on the left side of the forehead.

For thirty hours the carnage lasted, and all that time the wounded lay without a drop of water to quench their awful thirst. Then when deliverance came they were carried back to the fort, many of them to die. I know not whether his name is engraved on any monument which commemorates the deeds wrought by those brave men, but it will live in the hearts of those who knew him and loved him best. I would also add that the Indian, Ton-wan-I-ton, or Lorenzo Lawrence, who brought us to the fort, was taken into Gen. Sibley's employ as scout and returned with him, guiding and directing them to the enemy. The general came to see me in regard to their numbers and position and the probability of getting the captives. I referred him to Lorenzo as perfectly reliable and trustworthy, and he did not fail to fill the recommendation. The poor fellow was sadly wounded at the battle of Wood Lake, but never got a pension so far as I know.

He and his wife came to visit us at Fort Ridgley after I returned there and he made us several visits afterward. Whether he is now living I do not know, but for his faithful kindness to me and mine I shall never cease to remember him as a true friend, albeit an Indian, and one who did not fear to sacrifice all he had for the safety of his white friends. There were many others I could mention as deserving the highest praise for their devotion to the whites and but for whom many who were afterward restored to friends would have been of the number whose bones may even now be bleaching in some lonely spot. To such as those I owed my safety from dishonour and death.

I leave this imperfectly written sketch to the mercy of my kind friends, who, I trust, will understand how hard a task it has been for me to live over those unhappy days which are here recorded and which for many years I have striven to forget; and to all those who are now living that befriended me in those days of adversity I tender my heartfelt thanks, and, in the language of Wabasha, "I shake hands."

J. E. De C. Sweet.

Centreville, March 14, 1893.

The Story of Mary Schwandt

I was born in the district of Brandenburg, near Berlin, Germany, in March, 1848. My parents were John and Christina Schwandt. In 1858, when I was ten years of age, our family came to America and settled near Ripon, Wis. Here we lived about four years. In the early spring of 1862 we came to Minnesota and journeyed up the beautiful valley of the Minnesota river to above the mouth of Beaver creek and above where the town of Beaver Falls now stands, and somewhere near a small stream, which I think was called Honey Creek,—though it may have been known as Sacred Heart,—my father took up a claim, built a house and settled. His land was, I think, all in the Minnesota bottom or valley, extending from the bluff on the north side to the river. Our family at this time consisted of my father and mother; my sister Caroline, aged nineteen, and her husband, John Waltz; myself, aged fourteen; my brothers, August, Frederick and Christian, aged respectively ten, six and four years, and a hired man named John Fross. We all lived together. My brother-in-law, Mr. Waltz, had taken up a claim and expected to remove to it as soon as he had made certain necessary improvements.

The greater part of the spring and summer was spent by the men in breaking the raw prairie and bottom lands so that the sod would be sufficiently rotted for the next season's planting. My father brought with him from Wisconsin some good horses and wagons and several head of cattle and other stock. He also brought a sum of money, the most of which was in gold. I remember that I have seen him counting the gold, and I once testified that I thought he had at least $400, but some of my relatives say that he had over f 2,000 when he came to Minnesota. He had brought some money from Germany, and he added to it when in Wisconsin.

Our situation in our new home was comfortable, and my father

Mary Schwandt-Schmidt

seemed well satisfied. It was a little lonely, for our nearest white neighbours were some distance away. These were some German families, who lived to the northward of us, I believe, along the small stream which I remember was called Honey Creek. One of these families was named Lentz or Lantz, and at this time I cannot remember the names of the others. The country was wild, though it was very beautiful. We had no schools or churches, and did not see many white people, and we children were often lonesome and longed for companions.

Just across the river, to the south of us, a few miles away, was the Indian village of the chief of Shakopee. The Indians visited us almost every day, but they were not company for us. Their ways were so strange that they were disagreeable to me. They were always begging, but otherwise were well behaved. We treated them kindly, and tried the best we knew to keep their good will. I remember well the first Indians we saw in Minnesota. It was near Fort Ridgely, when we were on our way into the country in our wagons. My sister, Mrs. Waltz, was much frightened at them. She cried and sobbed in her terror, and even hid herself in the wagon and would not look at them, so distressed was she. I have often wondered whether she did not then have a premonition of the dreadful fate she was destined to suffer at their cruel and brutal hands. In time I became accustomed to the Indians, and had no real fear of them.

About the 1st of August a Mr. Le Grand Davis came to our house in search of a girl to go to the house of Mr. J. B. Reynolds, who lived on the south side of the river on the bluff, just above the mouth of the Redwood, and assist Mrs. Reynolds in the housework. Mr. Reynolds lived on the main road, between the lower and Yellow Medicine agencies, and kept a sort of stopping place for travellers. I was young, but rather well developed for a girl of fourteen and a half years, and I could do most kinds of housework as well as many a young woman older than I, and I was so lonesome that I begged my mother to let me go and take the place. She and all the rest of the family were opposed to my going, but I insisted, and at last they let me have my way.

I do not think the wages I was to receive were any consideration; indeed, I do not know what they were. Mr. Davis said there were two other girls at the Reynolds house, and that the family was very nice, and these inducements influenced me. So I packed a few of my things together and was soon ready. My mother and sister seemed to feel badly about my going, but I was light-hearted, and said to them: "Why is it as if I were going back to the old country, or somewhere else a long way off, that you act so, when it is not very far and I shall come back soon, and it is best for me, since I am of little help to you here."

So, at last we bade one another goodbye, and I went away down the beautiful valley, never to see my good father nor my precious mother nor my lovely sister nor my two dear little brothers anymore any more in this life. How little did I think, as I rode away from home, that I should not see it again, and that in less than a month of all that peaceful and happy household but one of its members—my dear, brave brother—should be left to me. Many years afterward my husband and I visited the region of my former home, and I tried hard to locate its site. But the times had changed, and the country had changed. There were new faces, new scenes and new features, and so many of them, and such a flood of sorrowful recollections came over me, that I was bewildered, and could recognize but few of the old landmarks, and I came away unable to determine where our house stood, or even which had been my father's land.

When I came to Mr. Reynolds' house I was welcomed and made at home. The inmates of the house at the time, besides Mr. Reynolds, were his wife, Mrs. Valencia Reynolds, and their two children; Mr. Davis, who was staying here temporarily; William Landmeier, a hired man; Miss Mattie Williams of Painesville, Ohio, a niece of Mr. and Mrs. Reynolds; Mary Anderson, a Swedish girl, whose father had been a blacksmith in the employ of the government at one of the agencies,' and myself. In a narrative, published by Mrs. Reynolds (now dead), which I have seen, she mentions a boy that lived with them, but somehow I cannot remember him.

I do not now recall anything of special importance that occurred during my stay here until the dreadful morning of the outbreak. Mr. and Mrs. Reynolds had been in charge of the government school for the Indians which had been established at Shakopee's village, only a mile away. Travellers frequently stopped at the house, Mattie and Mary were very companionable, and I was not lonesome, and the time passed pleasantly. I was so young and girlish then that I took little notice of anything that did not concern me, but I know that there was no thought of the terrible things about to happen nor of any sort of danger.

The morning of Aug. 18 came. It was just such a morning as is often seen here in that month. The great red sun came up in the eastern sky, tinging all the clouds with crimson, and sending long, scarlet shafts of light up the green river valley and upon the golden bluffs on either side. It was a "red morning," and, as I think of it now, the words of an old German soldier's song that I had learned in my girlhood come to my mind and fitly describe it:

O, Morgen-roth! O, Morgen-roth!
Leuchtet mir zum fruehen todt, etc.
(O, morning red! O, morning red!
You shine upon my early death!)

It was Monday, and I think Mary Anderson and I were preparing for the week's washing. A wagon drove up from the west, in which were a Mr. Patoile, a trader, and another Frenchman from the Yellow Medicine agency, where Mr. Patoile's store was. They stopped for breakfast. While they were eating, a half-breed, named Antoine La Blaugh, who was living with John Mooer, another half-breed, not far away, came to the house and told Mr. Reynolds that Mr. Mooer had sent him to tell us that the Indians had broken out and had gone down to the lower agency, ten miles below, and across the river to the Beaver creek settlements to murder all the whites! A lot of squaws and an Indian man were already at the house.

The dreadful intelligence soon reached us girls, and we at once made preparations to fly. Mr. Patoile agreed to help us. Mr. Reynolds had a horse and buggy, and he began to harness his horse, having sent La Blaugh to tell Mr. Mooer to come over. Mr. Mooer came and told Mr. Reynolds to hasten his flight, and directed him what course to take. I was much excited, and it has been so long ago that I cannot remember the incidents of this time very clearly. I remember that Mr. and Mrs. Reynolds and the two children got into the buggy, and that we three girls got into Mr. Patoile's wagon with him and Mr. Davis and followed. We did not take many things with us. In our wagon was a feather bed and at least one trunk, belonging to Miss Williams. Mrs. Reynolds' statement says that the boy started with an ox team and was killed near Little Crow's village, but I cannot now remember about this. It is singular that I cannot well remember the Frenchman who was with Mr. Patoile, when, in my statement before the commission the following year, I gave full particulars regarding him, stating that he was on horseback, and how he was killed, etc. I cannot account for this discrepancy, except that I have often honestly and earnestly tried hard to forget all about that dreadful time, and only those recollections that I cannot put away, or that are not painful in their nature, remain in my memory. The hired man, Landnieier, would not leave with us.

79

He went down the river by himself and reached Fort Ridgely in safety that night. Mr. and Mrs. Reynolds also reached Fort Ridgely, taking with them two children of a Mr. Nairn that they picked up on the road.

Mr. Patoile was advised by Mr. Mooer to follow close after Mr. Reynolds in the buggy and not follow the road. But Mr. Patoile thought best to keep the road until we crossed the Redwood river. He then left the road and turned up Redwood some distance, and then struck out southeast across the great wide prairie. It seems to me now that we followed some sort of road across this prairie. When we had got about eight miles from the Redwood a mounted Indian overtook us and told us to turn back and go up to Big Stone lake, and that he would come up the next day and tell us what to do. I do not know his name, but he seemed very friendly and to mean well; yet I do not think it would have been better had we done as he directed.

At any rate, Mr. Patoile refused to return, and continued on, keeping to the right or south of the lower agency. At one time we were within two miles of the agency and could see the buildings very plainly. We now hoped that it was all a false alarm. It seemed that the agency had not been attacked, at least the buildings had not been burned, and our spirits returned somewhat. But soon after we saw a smoke in the direction of the agency, and then we were fearful and depressed again. And yet we thought we could escape if the horses could hold out, for they were getting tired, as Mr. Patoile had driven them pretty hard. We were trying to reach New Ulm, where we thought we would be entirely safe.

About the middle of the afternoon some Indians appeared to the left or north of us. They were mounted and at once began shooting arrows at us. Some of the arrows came into the wagon. We succeeded in dodging them, and we girls picked them up. Miss Williams secured some and asked Mary and me for ours, saying she meant to take them back to Ohio and show them to her friends as mementoes of her perilous experience. (In the record of my testimony before the claims commission of 1863 I am made to say that only one Indian shot these arrows, and that he took the Frenchman's horse, but it is impossible for me now to remember the incident in this way.)

When we arrived opposite Fort Ridgely which stood about half a mile from the north bank of the Minnesota—Mr. Patoile supposed we could not cross the river, as there was no ferry there, and we continued down on the road to New Ulm. The horses were now very tired, and we frequently got out and walked.

When we were within about eight miles of New Ulm and thought all serious danger was over, we met about fifty Indians coming from the direction of the town. They were mounted, and had wagons loaded with flour and all sorts of provisions and goods taken from the houses of the settlers. They were nearly naked, painted all over their bodies, and all of them seemed to be drunk, shouting and yelling and acting very riotously in every way. Two of them dashed forward to us, one on each side of the wagon, and ordered us to halt. Mr. Patoile turned the wagon to one side of the road, and all of us jumped out except him. As we, leaped out Mr. Davis said, "We are lost!"

The rest of the Indians came up and shot Mr. Patoile, four balls entering his body, and he fell dead from the wagon. I have a faint recollection of seeing him fall. He was a large man, as I remember him, and he fell heavily. Mr. Davis and we girls ran toward a slough where there was some high grass. The Indians began firing at us. Mr. Davis was killed. The Frenchman ran in another direction, but was shot and killed. Mary Anderson was shot in the back, the ball lodging near the surface of the groin or abdomen.

Some shots passed through my dress, but I was not hit. Miss Williams, too, was unhurt. I was running as fast as I could towards the slough, when two Indians caught me, one by each of my arms, and stopped me. An Indian caught Mattie Williams and tore off part of her "shaker" bonnet. Then another came, and the two led her back to the wagon. I was led back also. Mary Anderson was probably carried back. Mattie was put in a wagon with Mary, and I was placed in one driven by the negro Godfrey. It was nearly 4 o'clock, as I remember from a certain circumstance. The black wretch Godfrey had been with the Indians murdering and plundering, and about his waist were strung quite a number of watches. I learn that this old villain is now at Santee Agency, Neb. He gave evidence against the Indians who were hanged at Mankato, and so escaped their deserved fate. The Indians shouted and were very joyful over the great victory, and soon we were started off.

The wagon with Mattie and Mary went toward the lower agency, and the one I was in went off into the prairie. I asked Godfrey what they were going to do with me, and he said he did not know. He said they had chased Mr. and Mrs. Reynolds, and he believed had killed them. He said: "We are going out this way to look for our women, who are here somewhere." About three miles out we came to these squaws, who were sitting behind a little mound or hill on the prairie. They set up a joyful and noisy chattering as we approached, and when we stopped they ran to the wagons and took out bread and other articles. Here we remained about an hour, and the Indians dressed their hair, fixing it up with ribbons. When we came up to these Indians I asked Godfrey the time, and, looking at one of the watches, he replied, "It is 4 o'clock."

About 5 o'clock we started in the direction of the lower agency. Three hours later we arrived at the house of the chief, Wacouta, in his village, half a mile or so below the agency. Here I found Mrs. De Camp (now Mrs. Sweet), whose story was published in the *Pioneer Press* of July 15. As she has so well described the incidents of that dreadful night and the four following dreadful days, it seems unnecessary that I should repeat them; and, indeed, it is a relief to avoid the subject. Since it pleased God that we should all suffer as we did at this time, I pray him of his mercy to grant that all my memories of this period of my captivity may soon and forever pass away.

At about 11 o'clock in the night I arrived at Wacouta's house. Mattie and Mary were brought in. The ball was yet in Mary's body, and Wacouta tried to take it out, but I am sure that Mrs. Sweet is mistaken when she says he succeeded. He tried to, in all kindness, but it seemed to me that he was unwilling to cause her any more pain. At any rate, he gave up the attempt, and I remember well that the brave girl then took his knife from his hand, made an incision over the lump where the ball lay, took out first the wadding, which was of a green colour and looked like grass, and then removed the ball. I think after this Wacouta dressed the wound she had made by applying to it some wet cloths.

On the fourth day we were taken from Wacouta's, up to Little Crow's village, two miles above the agency. Mary Anderson died at 4 o'clock the following morning. I can never forget the incidents of her death. When we came we were given some cooked chicken. Mary ate of the meat and drank of the broth. Mattie and I were both with her, and watched her by turns. It rained hard that night, and the water ran under the tepee where we were, and Mary was wet and had no bedclothing or anything else to keep her dry and warm. When at Wacouta's she asked for a change of clothing, as her own were very bloody from her wounds. Wacouta gave her a black silk dress and a shawl, which some of his men had taken from some other white woman.

Mary was a rather large girl, and I remember that the waist of this dress was too small for her and would not meet or fasten. It was in this dress she died. She was very thirsty, and called often for water, but otherwise made no complaint and said but little. Before she died she prayed in Swedish. She had a plain gold ring on one of her fingers, and she asked us to give it to her mother, but after her death her finger was so swollen we could not remove the ring, and it was buried with her. I was awake when she died, and she passed away so gently that I did not know she was dead until Mattie began to prepare the face cloths. She was the first person whose death I had ever witnessed. The next morning she was buried. Joseph Campbell, a half-breed prisoner, assisted us in the burial. Her poor body was wrapped in a piece of tablecloth, and the Indians carried it to the grave, which was dug near Little Crow's house. The body was afterward disinterred and reburied at the lower agency. A likeness of a young man to whom she was to have been married we kept, and it was returned to him. Her own we gave to Mrs. Reynolds.

While in Little Crow's village I saw some of my father's cattle and many of our household goods in the hands of the Indians. I now knew that my family had been plundered, and I believed murdered. I was very, very wretched, and cared not how soon I too was killed. Mrs. Huggan, the half-breed woman whose experience as a prisoner has been printed in this paper, says she remembers me at this time, and that my eyes were always red and swollen from constant weeping. I presume this is true. But soon there came a time when I did not weep. I could not. The dreadful scenes I had witnessed, the sufferings that I had undergone, the almost certainty that my family had all been killed, and that I was alone in the world, and the belief that I was destined to witness other things as horrible as those I had seen, and that my career of suffering and misery had only begun, all came to my comprehension, and when I realized my utterly wretched, helpless and hopeless situation, for I did not think I would ever be released, I became as one paralyzed, and could hardly speak. Others of my fellow captives say they often spoke to me, but that I said but little, and went about like a sleepwalker.

I shall always remember Little Crow from an incident that happened while I was in his village. One day I was sitting quietly and shrinkingly by a *tepee* when he came along dressed in full chief's costume and looking very grand. Suddenly he jerked his *tomahawk* from his belt and sprang toward me with the weapon uplifted as if he meant to cleave my head in two. I remember, as well as if it were only an hour ago that he glared down upon me so savagely, that I thought he really would kill me; but I looked up at him, without any fear or care about my fate, and gazed quietly into his face without so much as winking my tear-swollen eyes. He brandished his tomahawk over me a few times, then laughed, put it back in his belt and walked away, still laughing and saying something in Indian, which, of course, I could not understand.

Of course he only meant to frighten me, but I do not think he was at all excusable for his conduct. He was a great chief, and some people say he had many noble traits of character, but I have another opinion of any man, savage or civilized, who will take for a subject of sport a poor, weak, defenceless, broken-hearted girl, a prisoner in his hands, who feels as if she could never smile again. A few days since I saw Little Crow's scalp among the relics of the Historical society, and may I be forgiven for the sin of feeling a satisfaction at the sight.

But now it pleased Providence to consider that my measure of suffering was nearly full. An old Indian woman called Wam-nu-ka-win (meaning a peculiarly shaped bead called barley corn, sometimes used to produce the sound in Indian rattles) took compassion on me and bought me of the Indian who claimed me, giving a pony for me. She gave me to her daughter, whose Indian name was Snana (ringing sound), but the whites called her Maggie, and who was the wife of Wa-kin-yan Weste, or Good Thunder. Maggie was one of the handsomest Indian women I ever saw, and one of the best. She had been educated and was a Christian. She could speak English fluently (but never liked to), and she could read and write. She had an Episcopal prayer book, and often read it, so that Mrs. Sweet is mistaken in her belief that Mrs. Hunter had the only prayer book in the camp.

Maggie and her mother were both very kind to me, and Maggie could not have treated me more tenderly if I had been her daughter. Often and often she preserved me from danger, and sometimes, I think, she saved my life. Many a time, when the savage and brutal Indians were threatening to kill all the prisoners, and it was feared they would, she and her mother hid me, piling blankets and buffalo robes upon me until I would be nearly smothered, and then they would tell everybody that I had left them. Late one night, when we were all asleep, Maggie in one corner of the tent, her mother in another, and I in another, some drunken young hoodlums came in. Maggie sprang up as swiftly as a tigress defending her young, and almost as fierce, and ordered them out. A hot quarrel resulted. They seemed determined to take me away or kill me, but Maggie was just as determined to protect me. I lay in my little couch, trembling in fear and praying for help, and at last good, brave Maggie drove the villains away.

Mr. Good Thunder was not there that night, but I do not know where he was. I have not much to say about him. He often took his gun, mounted his horse, and rode away, and would be absent for some time, but I never saw him with his face painted or with a war party. He is living at Birch Coulie agency now, but Maggie is not his present wife. I learn that she is somewhere in Nebraska, but wherever you are, Maggie, I want you to know that the little captive German girl you so often befriended and shielded from harm loves you still for your kindness and care, and she prays God to bless you and reward you in this life and that to come. I was told to call Mr. Good Thunder and Maggie "father" and "mother," and I did so. It was best, for then some of the Indians seemed to think I had been adopted into the tribe.

But Maggie never relaxed her watchful care over me, and forbade my going about the camp alone or hardly anywhere out of her sight. I was with her nearly all the time after I went to live with her. She gave me a clean white blanket, but it was not white very long, and made me squaw clothes and embroidered for me a most beautiful pair of white *moccasins*, and I put them on in place of the clothing I wore when I was captured. Old Wam-nu-ka was always very good to me, too. The kind old creature has been dead many years, and Heaven grant that she is in peace. For several days after I first came to live with them they were very attentive, waking me for breakfast, and bringing me soap, water and a towel, and showing me many other considerations.

I think we remained at Little Crow's village about a week, when we moved in haste up toward Yellow Medicine about fifteen miles and encamped. The next morning there was an alarm that the white soldiers were coming. Maggie woke me, took off my squaw clothes and dressed me in my own. But the soldiers did not come, and we went on to Yellow Medicine, where we arrived about noon. On the way there was another alarm that the soldiers were coming, and there was great confusion. Some ran off into the prairie and scattered in all directions, while others pushed the teams as fast as they could be driven.

Four miles from Yellow Medicine I was made to get out of the wagon and walk. From this time every day there was an alarm of some kind. One day the soldiers were said to be coming; the next day all the prisoners were to be killed, etc. On one occasion a woman was killed while trying to escape. I was again dressed in Indian garments. I was told that the Sissetons were coming down from Big Stone Lake, and there was danger of my being killed if I looked like a white girl. Maggie and her mother wanted to paint my face and put rings in my ears so that I would look more like a squaw, but I refused the proposition. I assisted my Indian "mother" with her work, carried water, baked bread—when we had any—and tried to make myself useful to her. We lived chiefly on beef and potatoes; often we had no bread.

We were encamped at Yellow Medicine at least two weeks. Then we left and went on west, making so many removals that I cannot remember them. I did not go about the camps alone, and I knew nothing of what was going on outside. I saw the warriors constantly going and coming, but I knew nothing of their military movements and projects. A simple little German *mädchen* of fourteen cannot be expected to understand such things. I did not hear the cannon at Wood lake, and did not know the battle was in progress till it was all over. During my captivity I saw very many dreadful scenes and sickening sights, but I need not describe them.

Once I saw a little white girl of not more than five years, whose head had been cut and gashed with knives until it was a mass of wounds. I think this child was saved, but I do not know who she was. I do not remember that I talked with my fellow prisoners. I remember Mrs. Dr. Wakefield and Mrs. Adams. They were painted and decorated and dressed in full Indian costume, and seemed proud of it. They were usually in good spirits, laughing and joking, and appeared to enjoy their new life. The rest of us disliked their conduct, and would have but little to do with them. Mrs. Adams was a handsome young woman, talented and educated, but she told me she saw her husband murdered, and that the Indian she was then living with had dashed out her baby's brains before her eyes. And yet she seemed perfectly happy and contented with him !

At last came Camp Release and our deliverance by the soldiers under Gen. Sibley. That story is well known. I remember how angry the soldiers were at the Indians who surrendered there, and how eager they were to be turned loose upon the vile and bloody wretches. I testified before the military commission that tried the Indians. Soon after I was taken below to St. Peter, where I learned the particulars of the sad fate of my family. I must be excused from giving the particulars of their atrocious murders. All were murdered at our home but my brother August, His head was split with a *tomahawk*, and he was left senseless for dead, but he recovered consciousness, and finally, though he was but ten years of age, succeeded in escaping to Fort Ridgely. On the way he found a child, five years old, and carried it several miles, when, by the direction of a German woman he had fallen in with, he left it in a house eighteen miles from the fort. The child was recovered at Camp Release, but it was so much injured by wounds and exposure that it died soon after reaching Fort Ridgely. August is now a hardware merchant in Portland, Oregon.

Soon after arriving at St. Peter I was sent to my friends and relatives in Wisconsin, and here I met my brother August. It was a sad meeting for the two little orphans, though we were most happy in seeing each other. The next year I returned to Minnesota and testified before what was called the claims commission. The government had suspended the annuities usually paid the Sioux, and directed that the money should be paid to the people whose property had been destroyed by the Indians during the outbreak, or to their heirs.

An administrator was appointed for my father's estate, and a guardian for me and my brother. I testified to the property my father had, all of which had been taken or destroyed by the Indians; but I do not remember that my brother and I ever received but an insignificant sum, and yet I do not know why we did not. It seems that everybody else, traders and all, were paid in full. Some gold was taken from the dead body of an Indian during the war, and, from the circumstances, Gen. Sibley thought the money had been taken from my father. The amount was $90, but there was a premium on gold at the time.'

Gen. Sibley purchased two $50 government bonds with the money and held them for my brother and me some years. In 1866 Gen. Sibley gave me one of the bonds and $20 in interest on it, and my receipts to him for this money are among the Sibley papers in the Historical society. A part of the year 1863 I was with the family of my old employer, Mr. Reynolds, who then kept a hotel at St. Peter. In the fall I went to Fairwater, Wis., and remained with an uncle for two years. In 1866 I married Mr. William Schmidt, then and for many years afterward one of the business men of St. Paul. We lived in St. Paul until 1889, when we removed to Portland, Ore.

Two months since we returned to St. Paul. We have three living children, a daughter and two sons; four children are dead. Life is made up of shadow and shine. I sometimes think I have had more than my share of sorrow and suffering, but I bear in mind that I have seen much of the agreeable side of life, too. A third of a century almost has passed since the period of my great bereavement and of my captivity. The memory of that period, with all its hideous features, often rises before me, but I put it down. I have called it up at this time because kind friends have assured me that my experience is a part of a leading incident in the history of Minnesota that ought to be given to the world. In the hope that what I have written may serve to inform the present and future generations what some of the pioneers of Minnesota underwent in their efforts to settle and civilize our great state, I submit my plain and imperfect story.

Mary Schwandt-Schmidt.

St. Paul, July 26, 1894.

Mrs Caroline Harris's Narrative

It was by the alluring prospects held out by the Texian land speculators, that my husband, Richard Harris, together with our near neighbours, (Mr. Charles Plummer, and family,) were induced; in the Spring
of 1835, to dispose of their farms (situated in Franklin County, State of
New York) to bid a final *adieu* to their native homes, and commence
a long and tedious journey to Texas. For a journey so far distant, and
withal so expensive, my husband was but poorly provided; being possessed of but little ready money, (the produce, in part, of his farm,) and
his friend and neighbour, in this respect but in little better condition;
and myself, at that period, enjoying but a feeble state of health, and
burdened with the care of a tender infant, less than five months old.

It was in the month of May that we commenced and pursued a
route recommended to my husband, as the most safe and expeditious, (to wit:) first proceeding by way of the lakes and Ohio River
to Cincinnati, from thence down the river to New Orleans; and from
thence, by an overland passage to Texas, the place of our destination;
and although, after a passage of some weeks, we succeeded in reaching
New Orleans in safety, yet in the attempt of making the last passage
mentioned, our sufferings were beyond the power of human conception; and which, finally, proved fatal to every member of both families,
with the exception of myself, and my not less unfortunate companion in misery, (Mrs. Plummer,) whose lives, as the reader will learn,
were spared to endure afflictions that can be better imagined than
described.

In our attempt to reach the newly settled parts of Texas, by the
route recommended to my husband, after leaving New Orleans we
missed our way by following an Indian track, leading far west of Nacogdoches, and finally to a country wild and uncultivated, and inhabited by wandering tribes of Indians.

After crossing the Sabine River, we travelled several days and nights with a slow pace, and with great difficulty and fatigue; sometimes labouring over steep and lofty hills, and at other times through swamps and extensive marshes; and in addition to which, we suffered much by day from excessive heat, as well as from the bites and stings of the mosquitoes, sand flies, and a numerous host of other winged insects peculiar to that climate. We thus continued to travel, pursuing a north-west course until early in the morning of the 20th August, when, as we had let our horses loose to graze, and were ourselves seated in mournful silence beneath the shade of a wide branching hemlock, partaking of almost the last of the humble fare with which we were provided, the sound of the trampling of horses' feet were distinctly heard, and apparently approaching the spot we then occupied; and before we had time to seek another and better hiding place, we were surprised and surrounded by a very considerable body of Indians, mounted on horseback; who, perceiving our defenceless situation, with discordant whoops and yells, dismounted, and made prisoners of us all.

Although in our endeavours to reach some white settlement, we had suffered much, the twelve days that we had been travelling through what we had supposed, until now, a wilderness, uninhabited by any human beings but ourselves; yet, to this moment the life of my tender babe had been miraculously preserved!—and, although now a captive, that the little innocence might be still spared to me, I most earnestly intreated of those in whose power we then were; but too soon I found that my entreaties for mercy were ineffectual with those whose savage breasts glowed not with a single spark of humanity.

My unfortunate husband, and his not less unfortunate friend, Plummer, were both strongly pinioned, and bound to a tree by the savages; who, having burnt our waggons and loaded their pack-horses with the most valuable of their contents, Mrs. Plummer and myself were seized, and being, stripped of our loose garments, were each mounted upon and secured to the backs of their horses; and, contrary to my expectations, my entreaties that my tender infant might not be taken from me, were yielded to; and it was still, for a little while longer, permitted to draw nourishment from its wretched mother's breast. The savages having finally arranged everything to their mind, preparatory to their departure for their settlement, (about one hundred and fifty miles distant,) they set out therefore, apparently very much elated with their good fortune in capturing, with other prisoners, two females, for whom (as we afterward learned) a considerable bounty had been promised them on their departure, by two of their young *sachems*, whose wives (or "squaws") we were destined to become.

My husband was, on peril of his life, forbidden to hold any conversation with me, and the same was enjoined upon Mrs. Plummer; and to prevent which, they were both compelled to travel, mostly on foot, in front of the main body of savages. Mrs. P. and myself were compelled to travel about an equal distance in the rear. Having proceeded in this manner for the space of three days (encamping nights within temporary huts,) the strength of my poor suffering babe began to fail; and when attempting to hush its pitiful moans, and to revive it by pressing it close to my bosom, it was torn from my arms by a savage brute, and thrown into a bunch of prickly pears!—and which cruel treatment was repeated until it became almost lifeless, when a rope was tied around its body, by which it was attached to the horn of the saddle on which I was riding (an awful spectacle, indeed, for a poor disconsolate mother to behold!) and where it remained until in the very agonies of death, when it was taken therefrom by the same unfeeling ruffian, and thrown on a prairie, and there left to be devoured by the vultures! Alas! is there a mother, whose heart is not callous to every tender feeling, that cannot have, at least, some faint conception of what my feelings must have been at that moment I

My husband, who had been an eyewitness of this unprecedented act of cruelty, and unable to withstand it, snapped in twain the cord with which he was bound; and in the attempt to hasten to the relief of his beloved child, was intercepted, and so unmercifully beat and maimed by his savage captors, as to compel him to desist from his humane object, and to leave the little sufferer to its fate! It was, however, some consolation to its wretched parents to know that its sufferings could not have been of very long duration.

The day following we reached a small Indian village, apparently inhabited by a tribe similar to that to which our captors belonged, as they not only resembled them in person, but their habits and manners appeared very similar. It was at this village that we tarried one night, and which was then inhabited principally by squaws and their papooses, and a few aged males; the younger class having left the morning previous oil an expedition west, in quest of provision, of which they appeared but poorly supplied.

It was at this village that we met with an aged white man, who, although a Mexican by birth, could speak some English, and who informed us that he was first taken prisoner by the savages, (several

91

years since,) but was soon after set at liberty, and since that period had voluntarily remained with them. He had been told that many tribes still further west could boast of more or less, captives, who (with the exception of the females) were treated with much severity; while the latter were treated with more lenity, being in most cases adopted by and compelled to cohabit with Indian chiefs or *sachems*! The reader can better judge than the writer can describe, what must have been her feelings on the reception of such woeful tidings as was communicated by the aged Mexican. Our only hope was, that he might, for some reason unknown, have misrepresented facts; but, alas! too soon did we find by what my unfortunate female companion, as well as myself, afterward experienced, that .he had exaggerated nothing! Nay, it proved with us even worse than what he had represented! We were likewise told by our informant that:

> . . . the savages by whom we were captured, were of the Camanche tribe, who lived a wandering life, and had maintained their independence against the powers of Spain and the Mexican, states for more than one hundred years; that they were very numerous, and more warlike and independent than any other tribe in America, and a terror to the inhabitants of the frontier provinces of Mexico; that they had plenty of excellent horses; and the warriors, when on an excursion, were always well mounted; that the food on which they principally subsisted, was smoked and dried flesh of wild stags, an animal with which the country farther west abounded; that our misfortune in falling into the hands of these savages might be imputed (after crossing the Sabine) to inclining our course too far west.

The food allowed us, was scarcely sufficient to sustain nature; but, on this account, we did not suffer so much as from excessive heat, and fatigue, produced by the manner in which we were compelled to travel; but my unfortunate husband, as well as his friend Plummer, suffered more in this respect than either of the other captives; for while we were allowed to ride the whole way on horseback, they were obliged to travel much on foot, over steep hills and extensive prairies of brambles, thorns, and various kinds of prickly plants! Indeed, I cannot furnish my readers with an account, day by day, of this difficult and fatiguing journey; but, as respected our savage masters, every mile seemed rather to exhilarate, than to diminish their strength or depress their spirits; for while we (whose miserable captives we were) were almost overcome by the hardships we had experienced, and by the dreadful forebodings of the awful fate that might yet attend us, the savages (who apparently delighted more in the affliction of torment than the alleviation of distress,) were, no doubt, much elated at the prospect of not only receiving their promised reward, but of enjoying the opportunity of displaying us, poor friendless mortals, as the trophies of their savage valour.

About noon of the fifth day from that of our capture, the Indian whoop was sounded by our captors, which we doubted not was intended as a signal to apprize their savage brethren of their destined village, of their near approach—as the whoop was almost instantaneously re-echoed by them! In about fifteen minutes afterwards we were met by a very considerable number of their Indian friends on horseback; and among whom, were, as we supposed, three or four chiefs, who were distinguished from the others by a cap of feathers, and other ornaments, with which they usually decorate themselves. Immediately on their arrival, both parties came to a halt, and dismounted; and after conversing with each other for a short time, I was approached and seized at the same moment by two young chiefs, and pulled off my horse! and said chiefs, having still hold of an arm each, continued pulling me with all their might in different directions, which caused me to shriek aloud with affright as well as with extreme pain, occasioned thereby!

My poor husband being a near witness to the harsh manner in which I was treated, and my helpless condition, once more succeeded in breaking asunder the cord or withes with which he was bound, and hastened to my assistance! but, in his endeavours to rescue me from their savage grasp, his right arm was nearly severed from his body by a blow from a *tomahawk*, held by one of the chiefs. Had it been the fate of the poor man to have been instantly dispatched, it would have been a great mercy; as he was immediately thereupon made the subject of most cruel torture! While unable to arise, and while the blood was gushing from his deep and ghastly wound, he was seized by two savages, and by them held in a standing position over a blazing fire until life became extinct!

This sight (at the very idea of which all but savages must shudder) afforded the highest diversion to his inhuman tormentors; who demonstrated their joy by correspondent yells and gesticulations! and, during the horrible transaction, the two young chiefs having loosed their hold of me, to settle their dispute at once, drew their knives, and after

93

IT WAS THE MISFORTUNE OF MRS. HARRIS, & HER UNFORTUNATE FEMALE COMPANION (SOON AFTER THE DEATHS OF THEIR HUSBANDS,) TO BE SEPARATED BY, AND COMPELLED TO BECOME THE COMPANIONS OF, AND TO COHABIT WITH, TWO DISGUSTING INDIAN CHIEFS, AND FROM WHOM THEY RECEIVED THE MOST CRUEL AND BEASTLY TREATMENT.

some dangerous thrusts at each other, they were separated by some older chiefs, who recommended that their pretended claims to me should be decided by lot! I being, as it appeared, the favourite choice of both—being twelve years younger than my unfortunate companion, (Mrs. Plummer,) who was too in a much more feeble state of health than myself. I was indeed at this moment so overcome by the shocking spectacle which I had just beheld, in the tragic death of my dear husband, as in a measure to impair my reason, and thereby render me quite indifferent as to what my fate might be! When I became myself, I found my left arm clasped with iron grasp by the hand of one of the young chiefs, and who was endeavouring to lead, or rather to drag me to the Indian village, situated less than half a mile distant.

Although my sufferings, in our long and tedious journey through a wild and pathless wilderness, had been such as no one of my sex probably ever before experienced, and my feelings (by a view of the tragic and painful death of my beloved husband and infant,) such as not to be described; yet they were not to be compared with what were at that moment produced by the awful certainty that I was about to be doomed to a yet more dreadful state of misery and wretchedness! When we reached the Indian village, I was almost stunned by the frightful whoops and yells of the savages by whom I was surrounded—and not until the crowd was in some measure dispersed (by heavy blows inflicted without respect to age or sex, by the savage by whom I was still led,) did I discover that my not less unfortunate companion (Mrs. Plummer) was in a situation similar to that of my own, she being held by the arm by another chief, and a few feet therefrom, lay her bleeding husband, apparently breathing his last! and her only surviving son, then about five years of age, held with savage grasp by him whom, in all probability, his unfortunate father had received his mortal wound!

From this moment I saw no more of Mrs. Plummer until near eleven months thereafter. As regarded myself, I was soon given to understand that the brutal treatment that I had anticipated, was to be more than realized!—that I was indeed to be adopted by, and compelled to cohabit with, a barbarous and bloodthirsty savage; and one whose murderous hands had, in all probability, been stained by the innocent blood of my murdered husband! If I ever felt a willingness, nay, an anxious desire, to be called hence to the world of spirits, it was at that moment! and ought such a wish to cause surprise, when there is not probably a Christian female on earth, who, placed in my situation,

95

that would not have preferred death to life! Yes, in its worst forms, to that of becoming the companion, and yielding to the fulsome embraces of a disgusting and detestable savage!

Alas! however revolting the idea, such, indeed, was my fate! for a poor, forlorn, and friendless captive, as I then was, there was no other alternative. Anything that would appear like resistance on my part, would only have subjected me to all the tortures that their inventive faculties could have given birth to!

Alas, how sudden and unexpected was the change of my condition in life; but about five months previous, I was blessed with a kind and indulging husband and a beloved babe; and enjoying happiness and contentment by the fireside of our peaceful dwelling, where there were none to molest or make us afraid; but, alas, at this instant, not only deprived of my beloved babe and its indulgent father, but myself a friendless captive, plunged into a state of inconceivable wretchedness!

Having often heard it remarked, that although the American savage delighted in acts of cruelty and revenge, so peculiar to his nature, yet that it was contrary to his disposition, ever by a gratification of a beastly passion to misuse or abuse such unfortunate females as should fall into his hands; I at first felt somewhat encouraged by the hope that the loss of liberty would be the most of which I should have cause to complain; but, alas! too soon did I find, by awful experience, that this opinion as regarded myself and unfortunate companion, was a mistaken one.

No attempts were however made to gratify a such like brutal propensity until after the performance of a mock ceremony of uniting me agreeable to their Indian custom to the ruthless savage whose companion I was to become.

Preparations for such a performance were made the day preceding that of my arrival at their village; on which occasion a great number of the principal warriors, with others, were invited to assemble early at the *wigwam* of him whose associate I was by compulsion to become.

The savages, as they arrived, seated themselves in a circle on a mound of turf prepared for the occasion; and while they were collecting, half a dozen or more of their squaws were employed in daubing my face, breast, and arms with vermilion, while others were as busily engaged in decorating my head with feathers of various kinds. This being completed. I was led, like a lamb to the slaughter, to the centre of the circle, by the young *sachem* by whom I was to be espoused! he being painted and decorated in a similar manner as myself.

In the centre of the circle I was met by one who appeared to be one of the most aged of the savages present, wrapped in an Indian blanket, and other ways decorated after the Indian manner; by him, it appeared, that the ceremonies on the occasion were to be performed, and in the manner following. First, taking my hand and placing it in that of the young Indian, and immediately thereupon taking from his the said young *sachem's* neck a string of small glass beads, and placing them around my own; at the same time muttering something in Indian which I could not understand; but, immediately thereupon every Indian and squaw composing the circle, instantly arose, and joining hands, began singing and dancing to and fro around us! continuing this until they became nearly or quite exhausted; when, at a signal given, they reassumed their seats—when the old and young *sachem*, seizing me each by a hand, commenced a song and dance, similar to that which had been just performed by their savage companions!

But such was the state of my mind at that moment, that they found me but little disposed to yield to their will, or to participate in such amusements!

Indeed, had a natural death and Christian burial been afterwards allowed me, I should at that moment have been more willing to have united my voice with theirs in chanting my funeral dirge! Finding that I was not to be easily removed from the spot but by force, to intimidate me the old Indian, seizing the *tomahawk* which hung by his side, made a motion therewith as if intending to dash out my brains! but finding that all would not do, that I remained still fearless, and quite indifferent as to what might be my fate, he gave directions to his Indian brethren once more to arise, and repeat their dance as before—and which was accompanied with still more hideous whoops and yells!

Having continued this with very little cessation for half an hour or more, they began to disperse, each to his own hut; when I was led, or rather dragged, by the young *sachem* to the one occupied by him, and where I was doomed to spend eleven months in a state of bondage and misery that beggars description! Being not only compelled to cohabit, but to yield to the beastly will of a savage brute!

I kept no written record, nor will my memory admit of my furnishing my leaders with a relation of the transactions of every day during the period of my captivity; a great part of which, in consequence of my sufferings in both body and mind, I was seriously indisposed and confined to the bed if it deserves the name, composed of dry moss and a few filthy Indian mats.

The savage in whose power misfortune had placed me, not only claimed me as his wife, but treated me as his menial servant whenever he had occasion so to do—compelled me to perform tasks that my feeble constitution would not admit of, while his own time was employed in fishing, the chase, and other favourite amusements.

Nine months from the time that I first became a tenant of his loathsome dwelling, being sent to the distance of four or five miles to bring home the hides of some wild animals that he had killed the day previous, I was met by an Indian on horseback, wearing the badge of a *sachem*, whom I did not recognize at first, but who manifested some gladness to see me; and in broken English invited me to accompany him to his *wigwam* then in view to see "my sister," his "white squaw."

Thinking that this might possibly be no other than my unfortunate companion in misery, Mrs. Plummer, and anxious to learn her situation if living, I accepted the invitation, and was conducted to his hovel, and into the presence of my friend, from whom I had been so long separated, and whose fate I had been so long ignorant of. But never did I before behold so great a change in the appearance of any human being in so short a period! I was no sooner beheld and recognized by her, than she, with hands uplifted, and with a heart-piercing shriek, swooned, and fell senseless to the floor! As soon as she recovered, and became in a measure composed, she gave me a minute and heart-rendering account of her trials and sufferings since the period of our separation; which had been, if possible, greater than my own!

She had been adopted, and compelled to cohabit with the savage with whom she then dwelt, and from whom she had received the most cruel treatment. Her little son but five years old had been taken from her, and conveyed she know not whither! and about six weeks after she look up her abode in the hut which she then occupied, she gave birth to another, which was killed by the merciless brute in whose power she was, the moment after its birth! From her I learned, for the first time, that the tribe by whom we were captured and still held in bondage, were but a remnant of a very large tribe which infested the country nearly as far to the north-west as Santa Fe—that the detached party had been induced to take up their quarters here for the express purpose of harassing, intercepting, and preventing the encroachments of the Spanish Mexicans, who, by treachery as well as by force of arms, had already deprived them of a valuable portion of their country, and driven them back into the interior.

This information had been communicated to her Mrs. Plummer by an Indian hunter, who, in consequence of his intercourse with a company of whites, engaged in a similar pursuit at the far west, had learned to speak the English language so perfectly as to be well understood; and it so happened as the reader will hereafter understand that by the will of Providence this same Indian was finally made instrumental in effecting our redemption. After a short, but very affecting interview with my unfortunate female friend, and with the promise, on the part of both, that we would as soon as possible again see each other, we separated.

I ought here to mention, that the garments with which we were clad when captured, having been worn to threads, Mrs. Plummer as well as myself had been presented with dresses; peculiar to those commonly worn by their squaws, comprised of a blue cloth cap, a pair of moccasins, and an Indian blanket each.

Having been unable to find the hide of the animal for which I had been sent, I was obliged to return without it, and to meet the frowns of my Indian companion (as he termed himself; but, as such, Heaven forbid that I should even acknowledge him!) yet although in one respect he proved himself a savage brute, and at whose approach I could not refrain from trembling; in other respects he never attempted to lay violent hands upon me unless when intoxicated and it was seldom he ever returned from an Indian *pow-wow*, or *carousal*, in any other condition; then it was that he would manifest all that savage jealousy and thirst for revenge so peculiar to their natures. At such times my only safety was in flight to some neighbouring swamp, where I remained secreted until he became sober.

Having been once despatched by him on an errand similar to that last mentioned, by pursuing a track leading in a different direction from that which I ought to have taken, I lost my way, and penetrated many miles into a dark and solitary forest, and where I remained wandering to and fro three days and two nights, without knowledge which course to take.—At the close of the third day, when nearly famished by reason of hunger and thirst, my ears was greeted by the well-known savage whoop proceeded from a south-eastern direction; believing it to be that of my savage master in pursuit of me, I endeavoured to answer in as loud a manner as possible, and soon had the satisfaction to hear the whoop repeated, and apparently at a shorter distance from me; which I again answered, and in a few moments thereafter I beheld two Indians at a short distance on a rise of ground (one my master) on the run toward me.

As soon as they found that I was the object that they were in pursuit of, I was by signs given to understand that it was by the sagacity peculiar only to the sons of the forest that I owed my deliverance! As it was by the close examination of the imprint produced by my *moccasins* upon the dry leaves that they were enabled to trace me, and to discover the course that I had taken!

There was on this occasion an uncommon degree of joy and satisfaction manifested by my Indian companion (so termed;) but whether it was to be imputed to a degree of genuine love and regard that he entertained for me, or the high value that he set upon me as one subservient to his will, and whom he had the right to barter away whenever an opportunity should present, I never knew, neither did I care much to know; for, in my view, he was still no other than the same savage barbarian—the vile murder of my husband!

Three months after my interview with my unfortunate friend, Mrs. Plummer, and about fifteen months from the time that I first became an inhabitant of the Indian village, which since that period had been and was still my abiding place, the savages commenced preparations for a remove back to that section of the country where dwelt the greater portion of their tribe, from which they had been detached for the purpose mentioned; and for which, a few days after everything having been made ready they took up their line of march.

Their *wigwams* having been constructed of the hides of bullocks, they were rolled up and secured to the backs of their pack-horses, as was their provision for the journey, and every other article of easy conveyance, and which was by them esteemed of sufficient value to transport to so great a distance.

It was on this occasion that I had another opportunity to meet with and converse with my sister captive Mrs. Plummer, and had too an opportunity to witness the harsh and cruel treatment which she received from the inhuman monster who professed to be her companion! who, for the most trifling fault, and more frequently for no fault at all, would beat and maim her in a most unmerciful manner; and in more than one instance in my presence to that degree as to cause her to fall prostrate to the ground from the horse on which she was riding.

And to such, and still more severe treatment, she informed me she had been made the unhappy subject ever since the period when it was her misfortune to fall into the hands of the savage brute! Although my affliction thus far had been very great, yet I have cause to believe that those of this truly unfortunate woman had been still greater. In addition to the loss of a kind and beloved husband butchered by the barbarians at the moment of attempting to afford her protection, she had been an eyewitness of the murder of her newly born babe, and while bemoaning the loss of her only son, but five years of age, who but a few weeks previous had been torn from her arms, and conveyed she knew not whither! Surely, in a more wretched condition no one of the human race male nor female could ever be placed! Indeed, human imagination can hardly figure to itself a more deplorable situation!

Mrs. Plummer as the writer has been recently informed is about preparing a *Narrative of her Captivity, Suffering, &c*, for the press; to that we would refer our readers for a more particular account of her heavy trials and afflictions.

The Indians, with their squaws and papooses (as well as Mrs. Plummer and myself) were all mounted on horses, but the trials and difficulties that we poor unfortunate captives had been subject to in our late journey through the wilderness, produced fearful apprehensions that we should be exposed to the same again, but very fortunately for us we were in this respect agreeably disappointed, as the country through which we passed was much less marshy and uneven, and more free from the impediments that had before obstructed our passage; and hence our savage masters were enabled to travel with more speed, and were but nine days from that of our departure in reaching the place of their destination.

We were here, as we had been before when within a short distance of the Indian village, met by a very considerable number of its inhabitants on horseback, who came to welcome the safe return of their brethren after an absence of several months. The tribe was apparently composed of many hundreds, and their habitations being but mean and contemptable huts, their wealth appeared to consist principally in the great number of horses which they possessed. It was at this village that I soon found that the situation of both myself and my companion in misery (Mrs. Plummer) was to be rendered, if possible, still more wretched; it was here that we for the first time learned that the two chiefs, with whom we had been compelled to cohabit, had some time previously been here untied (after the same manner that we had been espoused by them) to other female companions, and by whom we, having become the subjects of their jealousy and hatred, were treated in the most cruel manner—being, through their instigation, not only confined to a very scanty allowance of food of the meanest quality, but deprived of the privilege of reposing at night under one and the same roof, being compelled to occupy a very small portion of one improved as a stable for their horses. But whatever our treatment, we were obliged to submit, and that without a murmur.

We found at this village no other captives but ourselves; but in almost every wigwam or hut were displayed more or less human scalps, of those who had at some former period fallen victims to their barbarity; some apparently were those of very young children! all of which were carefully preserved, and displayed on public occasions as proofs of their valour.

About four months after we had been brought to this village, we were eyewitnesses to a scene which no pen can truly describe!—a small detached party of the Calmanchees having the week previous set out for the purpose of depredating on some of the small white settlements, they were defeated with the loss of three of their number killed; the survivors, on their return the day following, fell in with an aged and unarmed Mexican, whom they seized, bound, and brought to their village a prisoner.

This poor man they very soon determined to sacrifice in revenge for the loss they had sustained in the deaths of the three who had fallen by the hands of the whites.

The unfortunate prisoner was put to death after their savage manner, having been bound to a stake around which faggots were piled to the height of his breast, and set on fire, and, while writhing with the most agonizing pains, the merciless savages manifested their joy and satisfaction by whooping and dancing to and fro around the burning pile, which they continued to do until death put an end to their unhappy victim's sufferings.

Although the Calmanchees were, as they had been for many years, the avowed enemies of the Spaniards, and their descendants the native-born Mexicans, yet they appeared to harbour no hostile feelings toward the whites of other nations; hence the hunters of such not only ventured among them without fear of danger, but were generally treated with great hospitality.

Had not the savages, by whom we were first captured, supposed our husbands Mexicans, they no doubt would have shared a better fate; but the savages being unable either to speak or understand our language, and being unaccompanied by an interpreter, they (our husbands) were made the subjects of savage cruelty, and were finally put to death in the manner as described!

Almost two years had now passed since it was my misfortune (as well as that of my suffering companion,) to be doomed to a state of worse than bondage, in which time we had been made to drink of the cup of woe to its very dregs! and, to add to our misery, there was not as yet the most distant prospect of, nor could we reasonably indulge a hope, of being ever again restored to liberty; and, indeed, began to look forward to death as the only termination of our captivity. But, in this we were agreeably disappointed! At a moment unexpected, Heaven was pleased to send (in answer to our prayers) the long wished for relief!

One morning, to my very great surprise, I was visited and accosted by one who from his appearance and dialect I judged to be one of my own countrymen; and after a moment's conversation, to my inexpressible joy I found that I was correct in my conjectures—he proving a native of the state of Georgia, and one of that class whose time is employed in hunting the most valuable wild game of the forest. He was accompanied by the savage of whom mention is made in a preceding page as being the first of his countrymen met with whom we could converse in English.

It was from him that our kind friend and benefactor first learned our situation; and he (the Indian) volunteering his services as a guide, was conducted to the hut, a part of which I had been permitted to occupy.

My Indian master being present, and assenting to an application that I be allowed the liberty to accompany the white stranger to the hovel occupied by my unfortunate female friend (Mrs. Plummer,) we hastened thereto, to bear to her the joyful tidings of the prospect of our speedy deliverance—having been assured by him by whom I was accompanied, that, if in his power, he would effect our redemption before his departure.

We found the unhappy woman in a condition similar to that in which I had frequently found her, a prey to melancholy, and the subject of remorseless cruelty. After a short introduction, we, by his request, proceeded to furnish our friend and countryman with a brief narration of our capture, the cruel manner in which every member (with the exception of ourselves) of our unfortunate families had been put to death, and the barbarous treatment which we had since that melancholy period received from the savages! At which recital our friend appeared much affected, and again repeated his assurances that he would not leave us until the consent of the savages was on some terms or other obtained that we be allowed to accompany him on his return home! and which, thanks to Providence, he soon after happily effected, by paying to them the sum of four hundred dollars as the price of our redemption.

A few days after that on which we obtained our liberty, we were visited by two more of our countrymen, who were also hunters, and the friends and acquaintances of our deliverer.

Having made the necessary preparation, we set out with our friends (all mounted on valuable horses,) for the land of our birth—our once happy homes! The knowledge which our friendly guides had of the country through which we passed on our return, rendered our journey less irksome and more expeditious.

In little more than four weeks from the time of bidding *adieu* to a savage wilderness, without any very serious accident attending us, we reached New Orleans. When about to bid a final *adieu* to that cruel race of people by whom I had been almost two years held in bondage, and from whom I had received such inhuman treatment, I could not refrain from bursting into tears of joy! Still there were intervals (during the two or three first days of our journey,) when it seemed almost impossible that I was entirely free from the power of those merciless wretches! And was sometimes pained with the idea that unforeseen events might still detain me among them!

At New Orleans my suffering companion Mrs. Plummer was prevailed on by an old acquaintance to remain a few weeks for the improvement of her health, which had not only become much impaired, but by the ill usage and privations which she had been subject, was reduced almost to a skeleton! As regards myself, although by my great sufferings my health still remains much impaired, and my constitution so much broken as to render it very probable that I shall enjoy no better health until the day of my death, yet during the whole course of my captivity I bore my sufferings and privations with a great degree of fortitude.

Having by the will of Divine Providence arrived once more on Christian ground, and permitted once more to breathe free air, (although I have been prevailed on to take up my abode with an only sister, many miles from my native home,) I cannot fail to improve this last opportunity that I may ever have to express my sincere obligations to my friend and benefactor, who so humanely rescued me, as well as my suffering female companion, from the hands of the cruel savages.

I shall not attempt to describe, because I have not a power of speech equal to the task, the strong sentiments of gratitude with which such uncommon kindness and humanity affected me; and to conclude, I cannot refrain from expressing in some degree a portion of that regard which I profess sincerely to feel for the welfare of my fellow-beings, those especially, who are of my sex. I hope that they may not be led astray, but improve, by the unwise examples of others; and be not easily persuaded to part with their peaceful homes, where with little labour a comfortable subsistence might be acquired, to expose themselves and families, if not to the cruelty of merciless savages, to all the privations and hardships so generally attendant on those who seek a residence in a new and uncultivated wilderness.

Emigration has for two or three years past been the prevailing principle which has actuated not only the needy adventurer, but, in too many instances, has proved the cause of the ruin of families, once comfortably settled in a land where the conveniences of life amply abound. It is, indeed, true, as has been remarked by a late eminent writer that the soil, climate, and natural resources of the eastern and middle states, constitutes everything that can render life desirable; and, aided by industry and frugality, all the blessings that can be derived from competency and civilization may be enjoyed in this happy land of our ancestors.

Yet such appears to be the restless disposition of a portion of mankind, that, notwithstanding they may be nurtured in a country abounding with every necessary of life, too many appear to be dissatisfied, and leave a comfortable home, to seek after wealth and popularity in the trackless wilderness.

Such was indeed, the unwise choice of my poor unfortunate husband and his not less unfortunate neighbour, who, in hopes of acquiring an easier living, bade *adieu* to their peaceful homes, never again to revisit them, but to become the victims of the bloody *tomahawk!* Hence it is, that by yielding too readily to the persuasions, as well as alluring prospects which have been held out by those who manifest so great a disposition to sport with the credulity of their fellow beings, and who have latterly engaged so deeply in the speculations of the wild lands of the West, and of which many possess but doubtful titles, it has been my misfortune, in the short space of two years, not only to be dispossessed of a comfortable home, but to be bereaved, and in the most cruel manner, of a kind and indulgent husband and a much beloved darling child.

In bringing my affecting narrative to a conclusion, I have only to add that I have furnished my readers with as minute a detail of my trials and afflictions as my present circumstances will admit of; and here permit me to inquire, is it not sufficient to satisfy every reasonable person that I owe my life, as well as my restoration to liberty, to the interposition of a kind Providence?—True it is, that should it please the Father of mercies to visit his friends and followers with afflictions, even as great as those with which he has been pleased to visit me, the recollection that all events are under the disposal of infinite wisdom and goodness will repress the rising murmur, and diffuse a delightful calm through the soul far superior to the exultation that arises from earthly posterity.

Subject to the control of this Almighty Guardian, all the trials of life are designed to establish our faith, to increase our humble dependence, to perfect our love and fortify our patience: nor has my unfortunate friend and late companion in misery Mrs. Plummer less cause to be thankful that, amid all her trials and afflictions, her life has been still miraculously preserved—although at the time of her capture, in delicate circumstances and naturally of very slender constitution, yet she was not only doomed to become the companion of a savage of the most brutal disposition, but almost every day for the space of nearly two years the subject of his revengeful, as well as jealous and lustful passions! The narrative of Mrs. Plummer, which is now preparing for the press, and will be issued in a few days, will comprise a faithful, although sorrowful detail of her sufferings from the day of her capture to that of her liberation from savage bondage.

Caroline Harris.

CERTIFICATE

I Ebenezer C. Elfort, a native of Madison State of Georgia, hereby certify, that early in the fall of 1837, being in company with others at Santa Fe, for the purpose of purchasing furs, I was there informed by a Calmanchee Indian of the captivity of two of my unfortunate countrywomen, and who were still held in bondage by the savages; and by my request, was conducted by the said Indian to the *wigwams*, where were confined said unfortunate white women, and whom (as correctly narrated by Mrs. Harris) I succeeded in redeeming out of their hands, and restoring to liberty.

Capture and Providential Escape of Misses Frances and Almira Hall

NARRATIVE &C.

The preceding year (1832) will be long remembered as a year of much human distress, and a peculiarly unfortunate one for the American nation—for while many of her most populous cities have been visited by that dreadful disease, the cholera, and to which thousands have fallen victims, the merciless savages have been as industriously and fatally engaged in the work of human butchery on the frontiers.

In the month of May last, a considerable body of Indians (principally of the tribes of the Sacs and Foxes) having, as they professed, become dissatisfied with the encroachments of the whites, invaded and made a furious and unexpected attack upon the defenceless inhabitants of the frontier towns of Illinois. The first and most fatal was upon a small settlement on Indian Creek, running into Fox River, where were settled about twenty families, who, not being apprised of their approach, became an easy prey to their savage enemies—indeed so sudden and unexpected was the attack, that they were unalarmed until the savages with their tomahawks in hand, had entered their houses, and began the perpetration of the most inhuman barbarities!

No language can express the cruelties that were committed; in less than half an hour more than one half of the inhabitants were inhumanly butchered—they horribly mutilated both young and old, male and female, without distinction of age or sex! among the few whose lives were spared, and of whom they made prisoners, were two highly respectable young women (sisters) of the ages of 16 and 18.

As soon as the melancholy tidings of the horrid massacre were made known to the white inhabitants of the neighbouring settlements, a company of volunteers of about 270 in number, were hastily collected and sent in pursuit of the savages, whom they overtook near Sycamore Creek, and resolutely attacked, but were unfortunately repulsed by a force far superior to their own, and were compelled to retreat with the loss of 50 of their number—many of the Indians were killed, but as they carried off their dead, the exact number could not be ascertained; one only was found on the ground the succeeding day; he had received a mortal wound, and in the agonies of death, had tomahawked one of the whites and cut his head half off, dying in the very act; his last convulsive struggle being an embrace of his enemy even in death! The bodies of the slain whites were cut and mangled in the most cruel manner that savage barbarity could devise; their hearts taken out and their heads cut off!

Immediately on the receipt of the melancholy news of the defeat of the volunteers, Governor Reynolds issued his proclamation, and a very formidable force (comprised of about 1400 men) were speedily raised, and under command of the Governor and Gen. Atkinson, marched forthwith in pursuit of the murderous foe, but were unable to overtake them, as it appears by the reports of the captives, who have since been ransomed, that after their engagement with the volunteers (the better to evade the pursuit of the whites) they separated into small parties, and fled in different directions.

The two unfortunates females, whom they retained as prisoners, and whose unfortunate parents were among those who were inhumanly butchered at Indian Creek, were providentially (by the aid of the Winebagoes) rescued from the hands of the savage monsters, after having been ten days in their power; in which time they were compelled to travel many miles, either on horseback or on foot, through almost impenetrable forests, and subjected to great privations and hardships, and in the expectation at every step in having their heads severed from their bodies, by the bloody tomahawk.

The third day after their engagement with the volunteers, and while on their return to their settlement, they fell in with a Kentuckian hunter, a young man of about 24 years of age, whom, after a consultation among themselves, whether they would dispatch him on the spot, or reserve him for other purposes, it was finally decided that his life should be spared until they reached the place of their destination, when and where (agreeable to his own statement) he was for 22 days made the subject of the most cruel treatment.

The report of the unfortunate young women (Misses Frances and Almira Hall) communicated to their friends and relatives, on their return from captivity, although treated with less severity, cannot fail to be read with much interest—they state, that after being compelled to witness, not only the savage butchery of their beloved parents, but to hear the heart-piercing screeches and dying groans of their expiring friends and neighbours, and the hideous yells of the furious assaulting savages, they were seized and mounted upon horses, to which they were secured by ropes, when the savages with an exulting shout, took up their line of march in Indian file, bending their course west; the horses on which the females were mounted, being each led by one of their number, while two more walked on each side with their blood-stained scalping knives and tomahawks, to support and to guard them—they thus travelled for many hours, with as much speed as possible, through a dark and almost impenetrable wood; when reaching a still more dark and gloomy swamp, they came to a halt.

A division of the plunder which they had brought from the ill fated settlement, and with which their stolen horses (nine in number) were loaded, here took place, each savage stowing away in his pack his proportionable share as he received it; but on nothing did they seem to set so great a value, or view with so much satisfaction, as the bleeding scalps which they had, ere life had become extinct, torn from the mangled heads of the expiring victims! the feelings of the unhappy prisoners at this moment, can be better judged than described, when they could not be insensible that among these scalps, these shocking proofs of savage cannibalism, were those of their beloved parents! but, their moans and bitter lamentations had no effect in moving or diverting for a moment, the savages from the business in which they had engaged, until it was completed; when, with as little delay as possible, and without giving themselves time to partake of any refreshment, (as the prisoners could perceive) they again set forward, and travelled with precipitancy until sunset, when they again halted, and prepared a temporary lodging for the night.

The poor unfortunate females, whose feelings as may be supposed, could be no other than such as bordered on distraction, and who had not ceased for a moment to weep most bitterly during the whole day, could not but believe that they were here destined to become the victims of savage outrage and abuse; and that their sufferings would soon terminate, as they would not (as they imagined) be permitted to live to see the light of another day! such were their impressions, and such their dreadful forebodings—human imagination can hardly picture to itself a more deplorable situation; but, in their conjectures, they happily found themselves mistaken, as on the approach of night, instead of being made the subjects of brutal outrage, as they had fearfully apprehended, a place separate from that occupied by the main body of the savages, was allotted them; where blankets were spread for them to lodge upon, guarded only by two aged squaws, who slept on each side of them.

With minds agitated with the most fearful apprehensions, as regarded their personal safety, and as solemnly impressed with the recollection of the awful scene which they had witnessed the morning previous, in the tragical death of their parents, they spent, as might be expected, a sleepless night; although the savages exhibited no disposition to harm or disturb them—early the morning ensuing, food was offered them, but in consequence of the disturbed state of their minds and almost constant weeping, they had become too weak and indisposed to partake of it, although nearly twenty hours had passed without their having received any sustenance.

The second day they passed much as the first, the Indians travelling with the same speed as on the former one; but nearly at its close, the two unfortunate females had become, through great fatigue and long fasting, too weak to support themselves longer on their horses, and were consequently dismounted and compelled to travel many miles on foot; and not until it was perceived by the savages that they were about to sink under the weight of their miseries, did they consent to come to a halt, and prepare quarters for a second night's lodging—a fire was kindled and some venison broth made, of which the unhappy prisoners were compelled by hunger to partake, and were then permitted to retire and spend the night as they had the preceding one, (as regarded any insult being offered them;) and being unable longer to resist the calls of nature, they the morning ensuing felt much relieved by the undisturbed repose which they had been permitted to enjoy.

During the long travel, or rather flight of the Indians the two preceding days, although they had in two or three instances met with small squads of armed savages, bound as was supposed to commit further depredations on the defenceless inhabitants of the frontier settlements, yet they had not until this the third day of their captivity, met with or beheld the face of any white inhabitant; when, at about noon, a Kentuckian hunter unfortunately fell into their hands; he was immediately seized and pinioned; and after nearly half an hour's consultation among those who appeared to be, chiefs, devising, as the prisoner concluded, the best plan to dispose of him, they again put forward, and a few hours before sunset, arrived at one of their Indian settlements, where, in consequence of their enfeebled and emaciated state, it was concluded that the two female captives should remain until recruited; and it was here that it was first communicated to them why their lives had been spared, and why they had been protected from insult, to wit: for the reason that they were to become the adopted wives of the two young chiefs by whom they were first seized!

If there was anything calculated to add more horror to their feelings, it was this, which was indeed calculated to produce a greater shock than the intelligence that they were doomed to become the victims of the most savage torture! Yet however great their afflictions, it was evident that they were supported and protected by that Supreme Being, who has power alone to soften the savage heart—*to break the chains of bondage, and bid the captive go free,*—for, although now completely in the power of the savages, and by everyone acknowledged the rightful property of two of their young and distinguished chiefs, yet for the seven days that they passed with them, they received none other but kind and civil treatment—the two young chiefs, to whom it was intended that they should be espoused, manifesting that regard for, and protecting them with as much interest, and apparent good feeling, as if they had been actually their lawfully wedded companions!

On the mornings of the 10th day from that of their capture, about fifty of the Winebagoes, (of a neighbouring tribe so called) who had been dispatched by the friends of the two young women, in quest of them, with means to ransom them if found alive, arrived—although the prisoners could not but feel overjoyed at this sudden and unexpected prospect of a deliverance, and to hail the tawny messengers as beings commissioned by Heaven, to rescue them from their perilous situation, yet they could not but discover, that on the minds of the two whose companions it was intended they should be, it had quite a different effect; and more particularly with one, who for some time manifested an unwillingness to receive any thing that could be named, in exchange for his highly prized captive! the ransom was however finally effected by adding ten horses more to the number already offered.

On parting with her, he insisted upon exercising the right of cutting from her head a lock of her hair, not as a relic which he was desirous to retain in remembrance of one, for whom he felt any uncommon degree of friendship and affection, but to be retained and interwoven into his belt, as an invaluable trophy of his warlike exploits!

such indeed is the Indian character—such their love of fame! The price paid in consideration of the ransom of the two female captives, was forty horses, together with a specified quantity of *wampum* and trinkets—the bargain closed, the prisoners were taken under the protection of the Winebagoes, and conveyed in safely to Galena (Illinois) and although they appear not insensible of the gratitude they owe to God, for their wonderful preservation and final deliverance from the hands of a merciless enemy, yet it is to be expected that they will long remember in sorrow, that fatal day, and the melancholy event, which not only deprived them of their liberty, but of their beloved parents, forever.

The Story of Nancy McClure

I was born at Mendota, then called St. Peters, in 1836. My father was Lieut. James McClure, an officer in the regular army stationed at Fort Snelling for several years. He was a native of Pennsylvania and graduated from the West Point Military academy in 1833, and was sent to Fort Snelling to join his regiment soon after. In the fall of 1837 he was ordered to Florida, and died at Fort Brooke, near Tampa Bay, in the month of April following, at the early age of twenty-six. Of course I cannot remember him, but from what my mother and others have told me, I feel very proud that I had such a father. He was a brave, gallant and noble man, and had he lived he probably would have made a good record, and my life would have been far different from what it has been. He married my mother at Fort Snelling, and she always cherished his memory.

Not long ago some letters of his were found among the papers of Gen. Sibley at St. Paul, and they show that he loved dearly my mother and me, his only child. I know very little of my relatives on my father's side. It is only lately, through the help of Gov. Marshall and another gentleman in St. Paul, that I have been able to hear directly from any of them, though I have tried for many years often and over again; but I am now in communication with them, and it gives me much happiness.

On my mother's side I know my family history pretty well. My great-great-grandfather was named Ta-te-mannee, or the Walking Wind. He was one of the principal chiefs of the great Sioux or Dakota Indian nation of Minnesota. My great-grandfather's name was Ma-ga-iyah-he, or the Alighting Goose. He was a sub-chief and a noted man. Of him *Neill's History of Minnesota*, giving an account of happenings at Fort Snelling in 1828, says:

One day this month (February) an old Sioux named Ma-ga-

NANCY McCLURE-HUGGAN

iyah-he visited the fort and produced a Spanish commission, dated A. D 1781, and signed by Col. Francisco Cruzat, military governor of Louisiana, the valley of the Minnesota at that time having been a portion of the Spanish domain, subsequently ceded to France.

I think it probable this commission had been given to my great-great-grandfather, the Walking Wind, and that he journeyed away down to St. Louis to receive it from his Spanish "Father." I do not, of course, know the circumstances, but would like to. The Indians greatly prize papers of this kind, and take good care of them, sometimes preserving them for many years. I have in my possession a paper given the Walking Wind in 1806, by Gov. William Clark, Indian commissioner. I am now trying to find the Spanish commission, and think I have discovered a trace of it. I know that some of my Indian relatives have some old papers, and I hope it is among them. But when I was a little girl my mother told me that once on a time, fifty years ago, some of my great-grandfather's brothers were drowned in a flood on the Missouri River. They were encamped on the river bottom, and during the night the water suddenly rose and swept them and nearly all the village away. It may be that they had this paper, and that it was lost with them.

The name of my mother's father was Manza-ku-te-niannee, or the Walking Shooting Iron—or gun. Another Indian of the same name, though commonly called Paul, was known to many of the old settlers and noted for his many services to the whites. My grandfather died when mother was about six years old, and she was raised by my grandmother. My mother's name was Winona, and my Indian name is also Winona, which, among the Sioux, means the first-born female child, and is as common a name among the Indians as Mary is among the white people. She was born at Redwood Falls. When she was young she was a very pretty woman, and very nice always. Before she met my father she was courted by two respectable mixed-blood gentlemen, Joseph Montreille and Antoine Renville, and Mr. Montreille wanted very badly to marry her; but the young white officer, my father, won her heart.

Two years after my father's death, though, she married Antoine Renville, and removed to Big Stone Lake. His father, Joseph Renville, was a very prominent trader in early days. There were three children by her second marriage Sophia,—now living at the Sisseton agency, South Dakota; Isaac, now a Presbyterian minister at that agency, and

William, now dead. My stepfather, Mr. Renville, always treated me very kindly, and I have nothing but respect for his memory. My dear mother died at Lac qui Parle in 1850, after a long illness. I was with her and cared for her a long time, and her death nearly broke my heart. My stepfather died a true Christian death in 1884.

Until I was about two years old I lived with my mother at Mendota, where I was born. Then my grandmother took me to live with her at Traverse des Sioux, and cared for me two years. Then, as mother was married again, and wished it so much, I went to live with her and my stepfather at Lac qui Parle, and my home was with them for ten years, or until my mother's death.

I had a pretty good start in the world for a poor little half-blood "*chineha*," if all the good intentions toward me had been carried out. By a treaty made with the Indians in 1837 the mixed-blood children were each to receive a considerable sum of money—$500, I think. My money, with that of some other children, was put into the hands of a man named B. F. Baker, the Indians called him "Blue Beard,"—a trader at Fort Snelling, to be held by him in trust for us. But in 1841 he went down the river and died at St. Louis, and that was the last of the money. I never got a cent of it. There is a record of all this matter, but there might as well not be. My father, when he was in Florida, wrote to Gen. Sibley, who was then at Mendota—but he was not a general then, only the head trader—and sent him money to provide for mother and me.

Then, when I was about eight years old, Mr. Martin McLeod—I think all the old settlers of Minnesota know who he was—began to give me clothing, one or two suits every year, out of his store. He said my father had loaned him some money, and when he was sent away, he (Mr. McLeod) could not pay him, and that my father told him to pay when he could, but to see that my mother and I were cared for, and if anything happened to my father the money was to be mine. I have forgotten the amount; I think it was $700, and yet that seems too large a sum. I do not pretend to know how much I got of it. After I was married Mr. McLeod came to see me and gave me what he said was the last of it, I think it was $15, but I am not certain. Of one thing I am certain—he gave me a good scolding for getting married.

When I was a very little girl, perhaps about eight years old, I was put to school. My mother was very anxious that I should be educated, and that I should become a good Christian. It was lucky that those noble men and women, the missionaries, had established schools among us at that early day, and were willing to make such sacrifices of their own comfort to instruct the Indians in the true way of life. I try to be grateful to those dear souls for what they did for me and others, and yet I feel that I can never be sufficiently so. The first school I attended was the Rev. Dr. Thomas Williamson's at Lac qui Parle. While here I was the only girl that boarded in the Doctor's household, and was treated as one of the family. Quite a number of the other Indian children attended the school during the day, but they went home to their parents at night. Some of them lived in lodges or "*tepees.*"

Dr. Williamson's sister taught us. I do not remember her full name; we always called her "Aunt Jane." They were most excellent people and true Christians. I attended this school for two years, when Dr. Williamson removed to another Indian village at Traverse des Sioux. Rev. Adams took Dr. Williamson's place as missionary at Lac qui Parle. When the Doctor and his family were about to leave Lac qui Parle they were very anxious to have me go with them, and I was just as anxious to go; but my mother was not willing I should leave her to go so far away. I stayed with them to the last minute, and when they were ready to start "Aunt Jane" said she would go part of the way home with me, for I had two miles to walk to my stepfather's house. She went about half the way, and then came the time for us to part. I was only a little girl, but I was in great distress and sorrow at losing my friend. She took my hands in hers and talked to me a long time. Then we kneeled down and she prayed long and earnestly; then we parted, and I ran home crying, and was the most miserable girl in the world, and I never saw dear "Aunt Jane" any more.

While at Dr. Williamson's school I had my first "Indian scare." How well I remember it! It was some time in the summer. The Doctor had some pretty young calves in a little yard near the house. He had three or four young children at this time, and we used to water these calves and care for them in other ways, and each of us claimed one. One day we heard an Indian coming toward the house, singing in a wild sort of way, and when we looked out we saw that he was drunk. He came up, jumped into the yard where the calves were, sprang at them like a panther, and killed every one of the little innocent creatures with his cruel knife. We were all terrified at the sickening sight, and screamed at the top of our voices.

My stepfather's house was not very far away, and I ran to it as fast as I could and told him. He came at once and stopped the wicked wretch from doing any further damage and drove him away. When the mother cows came home that evening and smelled the blood of their murdered offspring they filled the air with their wailings, and we children all had a good cry. I felt very wretched that night, but little did I think then that I was destined in after years to witness far more dreadful scenes.

After Dr. Williamson moved away I was sent to Jonas Pettijohn's school at Lac qui Parle. Here four of us mixed-blood girls boarded in the house. Rose Renville was one of them, and she was my roommate. The other two were named Caroline and Julia. I do not remember their family names; indeed I do not think they had any, except, perhaps, their Indian names. I attended this school for two years. Mrs. Riggs was our teacher. At these mission schools we girls were given religious instruction and taught reading, writing and something of the other lower branches, and to sew, knit, and, as we grew older, to spin, weave, cook and do all kinds of housework. We were taught first in Indian, then in English. I was not much of a little numskull, and I learned pretty fast and without much difficulty. My teachers were very kind to me—praised me and encouraged me, and I hope I did not give them very much trouble.

I remember another trouble we had while I was at Pettijohn's school. About this time the work of the missionaries among the Indians was beginning to show. A great many were joining the church and becoming good Christians. The Indians, who were still in heathenism—or belonged to the "medicine dance," as we called them—did not like this. One Sunday when we went to church, twenty or thirty "medicine" Indians, all armed, were at the building and calling out that they would take away the blankets from all who entered and destroy them. In those days every Indian who could get one wore a blanket. We girls had one apiece, and on Sundays, when we went to church, we took care to have a nice clean one to wrap our little brown forms in, and we were as proud of it as the grandest lady in the land can be to-day of her seal-skin.

I can tell you, too, that it was not an easy matter for an Indian to get a blanket, either. A good one cost f 5, and that was a big sum then. But the threats of the "medicine men" did not stop the Christian Indians from entering the church. They very readily gave up their blankets and went in to worship God, and to pray to him that he would soften the hearts of their wicked brethren outside and make them his servants, too. After we all got in and the services began, the men outside began to shoot at the church bell as at a target. They shot it several times, and actually cracked it so that it would not ring. Rev. S. R. Riggs was the preacher that day, and he was so affected that he cried before us all. Mr. Riggs suffered many other insults from those Indians. He lived in the next house to Mr. Pettijohn's, only a few steps away. One day in winter he was hauling wood with an ox team, and some Indians came and shot the oxen while they were hitched to the load. I think this was all the team Mr. Riggs had at the time. The Indians acted very badly, and I thought they would kill the people next, but after they had cut up the meat so that they could carry it they took it and went away. It was in the winter, as I have said, and meat was scarce and could not well be had without going out on the plains where the buffalo were, and it was easier to kill the missionary's oxen than to do that.

When I left Mr. Pettijohn's school I went home to take care of my mother, who was sick. As she was confined to her bed so long, I did not get to return to school for some time. Her death was a great blow to me, for we were much attached to each other, and now I was left alone in the world, an orphan girl of fourteen, with no one to care for me but my Indian relatives, and though they were kind enough, I did not wish to live with them. How much I longed to be with some of my father's people then, I cannot tell you. I was always more white than Indian in my tastes and sympathies, though I never had cause to blush for my Indian blood on account of the character of my family.

My mother knew my disposition and hopes and ambitions, and, on her death bed, she told me to either stay with my grandmother, who had raised her, or go to Rev. Mr. Hopkins, one of the missionaries, and not to stay with the Indians. During mother's illness Rev. Adams and his good wife, the missionaries at Lac qui Parle, came often to see her, and were most kind to her. When she died the body was dressed and prepared for burial by Mrs. Riggs, my former teacher, who was the wife of Rev. S. R. Riggs. Mr. and Mrs. Adams were here in 1891, and I had a good long talk with them over the old times. They live in St. Paul now.

So, after mother's death, I went to Mr. Hopkins and was taken into his school at Traverse des Sioux. I attended his school for about six months. His wife was my teacher. While here my intimate school-mates were Victoria Auge and her sister, Julia La Framboise, three mixed-blood girls, and Martha Riggs, a daughter of Rev. S. R. Riggs, the missionary. I learned very fast at this school, for I was now almost a woman. I was large for my age and strong and active. I could do all kinds of housework, and was a pretty good seamstress. My home was with my Indian grandmother, and I was the maid of all work. I was often flattered, and I am afraid I became a little vain. I know that I used to try to dress myself well and to appear well. I was fond of reading, and read what I could, but reading matter was scarce. One thing we had in plenty that I liked—flowers. The prairies were full of them, and I delighted to gather them.

In the summer of 1851 a great event happened at the Traverse des Sioux., This was the celebrated treaty between the government and the Indians, when the Sioux sold all their land in Minnesota to the whites. It was a grand affair. All the bands of Indians were there in great numbers. The commissioners came up, and with them a number of other white men, traders, attorneys, speculators, soldiers, etc. They had great times, to be sure, and I have always wondered how so much champagne got so far out on the frontier ! Gov. Ramsey was there, the governor of the new territory, a handsome man with a kindly face; he was a commissioner. Mr. Luke Lea, a one-legged man, was another commissioner. Another man with the commissioners was Mr. Hugh Tyler. He was a young man, very smart, with attractive manners, and a fine talker; he was there as an attorney for the traders, who were to get something by the treaty on old debts that the Indians owed them. Mr. Tyler came often to my grandmother's "*tepee*" to see me, and when he left he gave me a little Bible with his name in it.

Gov. Ramsey, too, came two or three times to see me. I remember well that he came once with Mr. Luke Lea. My grandmother and I had two tents, or "*tepees.*" One we used to cook and eat in, and the other was what might be called our parlour. The Governor and Mr. Lea came into the parlour tent, and, after a few minutes, they said: "Well, you are very nicely fixed here, but we don't see anything to eat." Then I laughed, because I saw that they thought we had but one tent and did not know of our kitchen; but I said nothing, though it was true that we did not have a very great supply. When they left, Gov. Ramsey told me to send my grandmother over to headquarters and he would give her some provisions. So she went over, and they gave her more good things than she could carry. I suppose that was what might be called an Indian trick played off on Gov. Ramsey.

Soon after this I was married. I was only about sixteen, and too young to marry, but nothing would do my lover but I must marry him, and I suppose many another woman, from her own experience, knows how it was. My husband was David Faribault, a son of John Baptiste Faribault, one of the first Frenchmen in Minnesota. He was a mixed-blood, a tall, fine looking man, and had a good reputation. He was a trader and very well-to-do for those days. I went to Gen. Sibley for advice on this subject, for we all looked up to him in those days and thought whatever he said was right. He advised me to marry Mr. Faribault, said he was a good man, a fine money-maker and would always treat me well. So at last I consented and the wedding day was set.

The wedding came off at the time of the treaty, and it was quite an occasion. There was a great crowd present, Indians and whites. I wore a pretty white bridal dress, white slippers and all the rest of the toilet, and I had taken pains to look so as to please my husband, and all those grand gentlemen crowded about me and made so many pretty speeches and paid me so many nice compliments that they quite turned my young and foolish head. Gov. Ramsey, Gen. Sibley, Mr. Lea, Mr. Tyler and all the rest were there, and some army officers, too, and so were the head chiefs and principal men of the great Sioux nation, and the affair even got into the papers. There was a wedding dinner, too, and somebody furnished wines and champagne for it, and I was toasted and drunk to, over and over again. I could do nothing in return for these compliments but bow my thanks, for I was a stout Presbyterian then and a teetotaller, and I would not take even the smallest sip of the lightest wine on any account.

About a month after my marriage a man came out from the East searching for me. He told me he had been sent by my father's people to take me back to them. I was much distressed. But I was a wife now, and my duty was with my husband, and I could not go. The man seemed disappointed when he found I was married, and would not talk to me or give me any information. I do not know who he was, but I heard that he died on his way back to Pennsylvania, or wherever he came from.

Two years after I was married I went down to St. Louis with my husband. He was going down to purchase a stock of goods and some horses. We went to St. Paul, and there took a steamboat, which was owned and commanded by Louis Robert. Mrs. Robert went with us, and we had such a delightful time throughout the trip. I saw so many things I had long wanted to see, the great city—though it really wasn't very great then—and the thousand other sights. On the boat, both going down and coming back, were a great many fine ladies and gentlemen, and they were all very kind to me. Indeed, the young Indian wife (I was only eighteen then) had far more attention than she deserved. In one thing I was disappointed. I had hoped that among so many people I would find someone that knew my father, but I did not. Mrs. Robert was my guide and kept me from becoming embarrassed, and I enjoyed myself so much. She and her husband have been dead some years, but I think all the people in St. Paul must know who they were, for they lived there so long, and there is a street in St. Paul named for Capt. Robert.

Sometime after my marriage my husband and I removed to Shakopee, where my husband continued in trade with the Indians for, I think, two years. He trusted the Indians to a large amount and they never paid him. Then we moved to Le Sueur and lived one year; then to Faribault, where we lived four years, and then to Redwood agency, where we were living at the time of the great Indian outbreak of August, 1862. Then it was that sad and hard times fell upon us and nearly crushed us.

At the time of the outbreak we were living two miles from the Redwood agency, on the road to Fort Ridgley. We had a log house, but it was large and roomy and very well furnished. When we first came my husband intended engaging in farming and stock raising, but he soon got back to his former business, trading with the Indians, and when they rose against the whites he had trusted them for very nearly everything he had, for they were very hard up, and the other stores would not trust them for anything. Besides the goods he sold them on credit, he let them have fourteen head of cattle for food. The winter and spring before had been very enjoyable to me.

There were a good many settlers in the country, some few French families among them, and the most of them were young married people of pleasant dispositions. We used frequently to meet at one another's houses in social gatherings, dancing parties and the like, and the time passed very pleasantly. I was twenty-five years of age then, had but one child and could go about when I wanted to, and I went frequently to these gatherings and came to know a good many people. Then came the summer, and the Indians came down to the agency to receive their annual payments under the treaty of 1851; but the paymaster with the money was delayed on the road until the time for the payment had passed. He was at Fort Ridgely with the money, all in gold, when the Indians rose. There were mutterings of trouble for some time, but at last it seemed the danger had passed away.

On the very morning of the outbreak my husband and I heard shooting in the direction of the agency, but supposed that the Indians were out shooting wild pigeons. As the shooting increased I went to the door once or twice and looked toward the agency, for there was something unusual about it. My husband was out attending to the milking. All at once a Frenchman named Martelle came galloping down the road from the agency, and, seeing me in the door, he called out : "Oh, Mrs. Faribault, the Indians are killing all the white people at the agency! Run away, run away quick!" He did not stop or slacken his speed, but waved his hand and called out as he passed. There was blood on his shirt, and I presume he was wounded.

My husband and I were not prepared for trouble of this kind. Our best horses and wagons were not at home. We had two horses in the stable and harness for them, but no wagon. My husband told me to get my saddle ready and we would go away on horseback, both of us being good riders. We were getting ready to do this when we saw a wagon, drawn by two yoke of oxen and loaded with people, coming down the road at a good trot. My husband said we would wait and see what these people would say. When they came up to us we saw there were five or six men, three or four women and some children, and they were all in great fright. They asked us to put our horses to their wagon—as they could travel faster than oxen—and to get in with them. This we agreed to do, and soon had the change made.

When they were harnessing the horses I ran to the house to try to secure some articles of value, for as yet we had taken nothing but what we had on our back, and I had many things I did not want to lose. Woman-like, I tried first to save my jewellery, which I kept in a strong drawer. This drawer was swelled and I could not open it, and I was running for an axe to burst it, when my husband said, "Let it go—they are ready to start." So I took my dear little daughter, who was eight years old and my only child, and we started for the wagon.

Just as I was about to get in—everybody else was in—I looked up the road toward the agency and saw the Indians coming. I was afraid they would overtake the wagon; so I declined to get in, and my husband got out with me, and we took our child and ran for the woods, while the wagon started off, the men lashing the horses every jump.

Just as we started for the woods, Louis Brisbois and his wife and two children, mixed-blood people, came up and went with us. We all hid in the wood. In a few minutes the Indians came up, and somehow they knew we were hidden, and they called out very loudly: "Oh, Faribault, if you are here, come out; we won't hurt you." My husband was armed and had determined to sell his life for all it would bring, and I had encouraged him; but now it seemed best that we should come out and surrender, and so we did. The Indians at once disarmed my husband. They seemed a little surprised to see the Brisbois family, and declared they would kill them, as they had not agreed to spare their lives. Poor Mrs. Brisbois ran to me and asked me to save her, and she and her husband got behind me, and I began to beg the Indians not to kill them. My husband asked the Indians what all this meant—what they were doing anyhow.

They replied, "We have killed all the white people at the agency; all the Indians are on the warpath; we are going to kill all the white people in Minnesota; we are not going to hurt you, for you have trusted us with goods, but we are going to kill these Brisbois." And then one ran up and struck over my shoulder and hit Mrs. Brisbois a cruel blow in the face, saying she had treated them badly at one time. Then I asked them to wait until I got away, as I did not want to see them killed. This stopped them for half a minute, when one said: "Come to the house." So we started for the house, and just then two more wagons drawn by oxen and loaded with white people came along the road. All the Indians left us and ran yelling and whooping to kill them.

We went into the house. At the back part of the house was a window, and a little beyond was a corn field. I opened the window and put the Brisbois family out of it, and they ran into the cornfield and escaped. They are living somewhere in Minnesota today. The white people were nearly all murdered. I could not bear to see the sickening sight, and so did not look out, but while the bloody work was being done an Irish woman named Hayden came running up to the house crying out for me to save her. I saw that she was being chased by a young Indian that had once worked for us, and I called to him to spare her, and he let her go. I heard that she escaped all right. Now, all this took place in less time than one can write about it.

When the killing was over the Indians came to the house and ordered us to get into one of the wagons and go with them back to the agency. This we did, my husband driving the team. The Indians drove the other team. Soon after we started an Indian gave me a colt to lead behind the wagon. About half way to the agency we saw the dead body of a man lying near the road. Just before we reached the ferry over the Minnesota River we saw a boy on the prairie to the right. There were but three Indians with us now. One of them ran to kill the boy. At this moment a German rode up to us. I have forgotten his name, but the Indians called him "Big Nose." I think he is living at Sleepy Eye, Minn., now.

One of the Indians said to the other Indian, "Shoot him and take his horse." The other said, "Wait till my son comes back and then we will kill him." (His son was the one that had gone to kill the boy.) All this time I was begging them not to kill the man. I asked my husband to plead with them, but he seemed to be unable to speak a word. At last I told the German to give them his horse and run into the brush. This he did and escaped.

When we got to the ferry the boat was in the middle of the stream, and standing upon it was a young white girl of about sixteen or seventeen years of age. The Indians called to her to bring the boat ashore, but she did not obey them. They were about to shoot her, when my husband told her they would kill her if she did not do as they ordered, and she brought the boat ashore. When it touched the bank a young Indian made this girl get on a horse behind him and he rode away with her, and I never heard what became of the poor creature. When I saw her being taken away I felt as badly as if she was being murdered before my eyes, for I imagined she would suffer a most horrible fate.

When we reached the agency there was a dreadful scene. Everything was in ruins, and dead bodies lay all about. The first body we saw was that of one of La Bathe's clerks. It lay by the road some distance from the buildings. The rest were nearer the buildings, Mr. Myrick's among them. We did not stay long here, but pushed on to Little Crow's camp. We stayed that night with the Indians that brought us. Soon other prisoners, many of them half-bloods like ourselves, were brought in.

While we were in this camp we saw, Capt. Marsh and his men coming from Fort Ridgley along the road towards the ferry. They could not see us, but we saw them, though at some distance. You know they were going to the agency, having heard that the Indians were rising. They stopped at our house and seemed to be getting water from the well. Poor fellows! Little did some of them think they were taking their last drink. They went on, and soon came to the ferry and fell into that bloody ambush where Capt. Marsh, Mr. Quinn and so many others were killed.

The next day the Indians under Little Crow went to attack Fort Ridgley. When they came back they reported that there were many half-breeds in the fort that fought against them, and shouted to them: "We will fix you, you devils; you will eat your children before winter."

This made them very bitter against us, for they said we were worse than the whites, and that they were going to kill all of us. Most of them had whisky, and it was a dreadful time. Towards evening a heavy storm came up, and a thunderbolt struck and killed an Indian. Someone raised a cry, "They are killing the half-breeds now!"

I caught up my child and ran. I saw my husband, with Alex Graham, running into Little Crow's cornfield, and I saw him no more that night. An Indian woman went with me, and we did not stop until we got to Shakopee's camp, seven miles away. It was Indians, any way, the best I could do, and I had some distant relatives in that camp, and I would rather trust myself there than with Little Crow's drunken and infuriated warriors. My friends treated me very kindly—gave me a dry blanket and some dry clothes for my little girl, who was quite sick by this time. It was an awful night. Towards midnight the Indians brought in a lot of captive white women and children, who cried and prayed the rest of the night. How I felt for them, but of course I could not help them.

The next morning I left my child with my Indian friends and I and the woman who had come with me went back to Little Crow's camp to see what had become of my husband and how things were. No one had been killed except the Indian who was struck by lightning. To our surprise we found my husband in the camp, and my companion's husband sitting over him very drunk, and with a butcher knife in his hand! The woman took the knife from her husband, and all was quiet for a time. My husband said he came back soon after we left, and that the Indian had been following him and threatening to kill him all night.

The team of horses we let the white people have at our house took them safely to Fort Ridgely. Just outside the fort one of the horses dropped dead. The other was left on the prairie, and the Indians that attacked the fort caught it. I think it was the fourth day of the outbreak that I was strolling through Little Crow's camp, when I saw my horse "Jerry" I untied him and was leading him away when an Indian ran up and said: "Here, I captured that horse at the fort, and he is mine." I told him I did not care how he got him; he was mine, and I was going to take him. At last he allowed me to have him. I had that horse at Camp Release, and took him with me to Faribault, Minn.

The funny part of this story is that this same Indian is living here, near Flandrau, now. About two years ago he wanted to borrow some money from one of the banks here and wanted me to go with him and recommend him to the bank. He said he thought I ought to go, as he let me take that horse !

Another day the cry was raised that the half-breeds were all to be killed. Little Crow held a council and would allow no Indians to attend it that had half-breed relatives. We thought this looked bad for us, and there were all sorts of alarming reports. Three young Indians came and sat by our camp and talked, and were heard to say that when the half-blood men were killed one of them should have me for his wife; I presume they meant the one that should murder my husband. A few minutes afterward my uncle, with three of his cousins, rode into the camp. My uncle's name was Rday-a-mannee (the Rattling Walker). He was a very brave, good man, and had taken no part in the outbreak. To my great joy, he said he had come to take us away.

When Little Crow heard this he came out and told my uncle that he would not allow anyone to take away half-bloods from the camp, and if any one tried to he would order his warriors to kill him. How proud I was of my brave uncle when he made this reply: "Little Crow, I only want the people who belong to me, and I will take them. You think you are brave because you have killed so many white people. You have surprised them; they were not prepared for you, and you know it. When we used to fight the Chippewas you were all women; you would not fight, If I leave these people here you will worry them to death. Now, I am going to take my people, and I would like to see the man that will try to stop me!" With this we started, and some of the Indians raised the war-whoop. But we kept on, my uncle and his cousins riding in the rear, their guns in their hands, and Little Crow and his warriors looking sullenly but silently at us.

The first day out we got as far as Yellow Medicine. From here we went to the mouth of the Chippewa River, where my uncle lived. Here I found my old grandmother, too, for she was the mother of Rday-a-mannee, and he and my own mother were full brother and sister. I now felt much better, and my appetite came back. Since the outbreak I had scarcely eaten anything. Grandmother died only a few years ago in Manitoba; she was very old. My uncle is still living in Manitoba. He was accused of taking part in the outbreak, I suppose, and that is why he left the United States. But I know he was innocent; if I knew he was not, I would be very sorry, but I would say so. Some of the Indians have been accused of taking part in that dreadful thing who are innocent; but a great many more are said to be innocent who are really guilty.

Some days after we got to the mouth of the Chippewa, Little Crow's and Shakopee's bands and all the other Indians came up. We all stayed here until Gen. Sibley and his troops came into the country, and then the Indians went out to meet them. In a few days we heard the booming of the cannon in the battle of Wood lake. Commonly the roar of cannon is a dreadful sound in the ears of women, but to us captives in the Indian camp the sound of Gen. Sibley's guns was as sweet as the chimes of wedding bells to the bride.

Very soon stragglers came in bearing wounded, singing the death song and telling the tale of defeat. They were cursing the half-breeds, saying that Gen. Sibley had numbers of them with him in the battle, and that every shot that one of them fired had hit an Indian. It did me real good to learn that so many of my race had stood loyal and true and had done such good service. You know that only a very few half-breeds took part in the outbreak. The Indians have always bitterly hated the half-breeds for their conduct in favour of the whites in that and other wars, and they hate them still. It seems they can forgive everybody but us.

But then came the word that the defeated Indians would take vengeance on the half-breed captives and the whites, too, as soon as they got back. It was another exciting time. Some of us dug holes in the ground and hid ourselves. I dug a hole large enough to hide myself and child in a few minutes, and I had only a little fire shovel to dig with, but I made the dirt fly. When the excitement was over—for the alarm was false—I tried again to dig with that same shovel, and somehow it wouldn't dig a little bit! I kept that shovel for years, but finally lost it.

When the warriors came back they had numbers of wounded, and the death song was going all night. I began to be very brave. The soldiers were near, the half-bloods were in the saddle and I felt that I would soon be safe. An Indian woman near me began abusing us. She said: "When we talk of killing these half-breeds they drop their heads and sneak around like a bird-dog." Her taunting speech stung me to the heart, and I flew at that woman and routed her so completely that she bore the marks for some time, and I am sure she remembered the lesson a great deal longer! Perhaps it was not a very ladylike thing to do, but I was dreadfully provoked. Most of my companions were greatly pleased, and the Indians did not offer to interfere.

I heard the Indians plan their part of the battle of Wood lake. About twenty of the chiefs and head warriors sat down near our tent one evening and talked it all over in my hearing. I do not now remember who all of them were. Little Crow was there, and with him were Pa-ji-ro-ta (Gray Grass), Hu-sap-sa-pa (Black Leg) and his brother, Ta-taka-wa-nagi (Buffalo Ghost), Shakopee (Six) and others. I did not understand the plan very well, but it was agreed that Gen. Sibley's forces were to be cut into two or three parts by the Indian movements. A strong party was to go into a large ravine. Another party was to show itself at another point and attract the attention of the soldiers; then the ravine party was to come up and cut the white forces in two, and so on. When I heard all this it did not alarm me the least bit. I knew that Gen. Sibley and Col. Marshall and Col. McPhail and the other officers would have something to say and do about that fight. But the Indians were confident, and, as they were leaving the camp, many of them said: "We will have plenty of pork and hard-tack tonight!"

At last Gen. Sibley came and surrounded our camp. A great many officers came with him, and I remember that Col. Marshall was one of them. They came into the camp and took away the white captives first. Gen. Sibley knew me, and told me to take my child and go with them. I asked him if all the half-bloods were going and he said they were not. I did not understand it all then, and I said I would stay awhile. Maj. Fowler, who was married to my husband's sister, then came and told me I had better go, as the soldiers were greatly enraged at some of the half-bloods, and their officers were afraid they could not "hold them."

I told him I had a half-brother and a half-sister there, and I would stay to protect them. So I stayed that night there, and went over into Camp Release in the morning. I was a witness before the military commission that tried the Indians, and called several times, but I could not recognize any of the prisoners as those I saw taking part in the murders of the whites. I was sorry that the guilty wretches I had seen were not brought up. I think I was at Camp Release about two weeks.

I cannot tell all of the scenes I saw while I was a captive. Some were very painful. I knew a great many of the white prisoners I was with, but now I only remember the names of Mrs. Crothers, Mrs. White and her daughter and Miss Williams. Some of the women came to me at times and asked me to let them stay with me. It was hard to refuse them, but I thought it best. I saw many women, some of them French women, that I had met the winter before at the country dances and other parties I have spoken of. I saw George H. Spencer quite often;

he was still suffering from his wounds.

The night before the troops came to Camp Release, twenty or thirty Indians came in with a young white girl of sixteen or seventeen. She was nearly heartbroken, and quite in despair. When the half-breed men saw her they determined to rescue her, and we women encouraged them. Joe Laframboise and nine other mixed bloods went boldly up and took the girl from her brutal captors. The Indians threatened to shoot her if she was taken from them; but Joe was very brave, and said: "We are going to have her if we have to fight for her; and if you harm her it will be the worse for you. Remember, we are not your prisoners anymore." So they took her, and she was rescued at Camp Release. Two other half-breed boys acted very bravely on this occasion—the Robertson boys; each was named Thomas, but they were not related. One of them is living at Sisseton; the other died five years ago, but his family lives near Flandrau.

One day Shakopee came to our camp and talked with me. He said he would not have taken part in the outbreak but for the fact that his son had gone off hunting and the whites had killed him. "And now," said he, "my arm is lame from killing white people." A few days afterward his son returned all safe. The only time I spoke to Little Crow was the day my uncle came for us. He ordered my husband to hitch up a team for him that he had taken. The horses were not well broken and were quite wild, and he could not hitch them up himself.

When we were at Camp Release a Mrs. Huggins, who had been the wife of Amos Huggins, who had been killed, lived near us. He and I were children together at Lac qui Parle. One day her little girl, three years of age, a bright child, came to our tent when my husband and I were eating dinner, and we gave her a seat with us. The little thing said: "This is not like the dinner mamma made the day papa was killed. The Indians killed my papa on his very birthday. We were going to have a good dinner. Mamma made a cake and everything nice, and papa came home with a load of hay, and the Indians shot him. But my papa isn't dead for sure. He is in heaven with God. You know, Mrs. Faribault, God is everywhere." We could not eat another bite after that.

I think the only time I laughed while I was a captive was at an Irish woman, another captive. She was about forty-five years of age and not very shapely of form. Just before Camp Release we made many moves of a mile or two. The Indians had taken her ox team, and had often let her ride on the marches; but on the last march they made her walk. She came to our camp and inquired of my husband for John Mooer.

She had on squaw clothes, had a baby in her arms, her face was very dirty, her hair tousled, and she was sputtering away in her Irish brogue and was a comical sight. She knew my husband, and she said: "Mr. Faribault, where are we goin' anyways?"

My husband said: "We are going to the whites pretty soon."

Then she said: "Well, I wish they would do something; I am sick of this campin' and trampin' all the time. That's my team they have, and the blackguards do be makin' me walk, and, be gosh, I am goin' to see John Mooer about it," and off she went to find Mr. Mooer.

While the Indians were away fighting at Wood lake, I and others of the mixed-bloods could have gone away from the camp; but Little Crow said if any of us did so those who remained should be killed; and so I thought it better to stay. Some women went away all the same, and escaped, too—Mrs. Quinn, Mrs. Prescott, with their children, and others. They seemed to know that Little Crow's threat was only a bluff, but he might have carried it out had he won that battle.

At last a lot of us released captives were started off for the settlements below. There were seven wagon loads of us in the party, whites and mixed-bloods, all women. At St. Peter's a store building was cleared out, cooking stoves put up, and bedding given us. An officer, whose name I am sorry I cannot remember, was in charge of us. Joe Coursalle, a noted half-blood scout, was with us. In the evening the German, whose life I saved the first day of the outbreak, came into the room. He was intoxicated, had a knife in his hand, and said he was looking for an Indian to kill. The officer had gone out, but Coursalle was in and said to the reckless fellow, pointing to me, "Here is the woman that saved your life." This seemed to quiet him, and he thanked me very kindly.

Then the officer came in and said to him: "Get out, you rascal. If you want to kill an Indian so bad, go West, to the front. There are lots of them out there, and they want to fight," and he put him out.

I went to Faribault and stayed at the home of my brother-in-law, Maj. Fowler, for some time. My husband remained with the troops under Gen. Sibley. All we had left was my horse, "Jerry." Our property had all been taken or destroyed by the Indians, but our log house was not burned. Our loss, besides what the Indians owed my husband, was fully $3,000. Our home was at Faribault for two years. We then moved back to Redwood, and then to Big Stone Lake. Here, through Mr. L. Quinn, the scout, who has always been my staunch friend, my husband got employment as interpreter under Maj. Grossman, who, with a party of soldiers, was on the way to build Fort Ransom, 150 miles northwest of Big Stone Lake. We reached the site of the new fort in June, 18G7. My husband was placed in charge of the scouts at this fort.

In the fall of 1867 we went out about thirty miles from the fort on the Cheyenne River and kept a mail station, where the horses of the mail coaches were changed. We also kept a house of entertainment for travellers. While here we had much trouble from the Indians. We were beginning to "pick up" a little after losing everything in the outbreak of 1862, when another loss came. In June, 1868, my husband went to Winnipeg—or Fort Garry—to put our daughter in school. While he was away the scouts rode up one day and told me that a strong Indian war party was not far off, and that we had better run away. I and others connected with the station got ready at once. Our wagon was not at home, and my husband had the buggy. We put some things into two carts and hid some other goods and went as fast as we could to Fort Abercrombie, forty miles away.

We stayed at Abercrombie two weeks, until my husband came; and when we went back home we found that everything had been taken by the Indians, even the things we had hidden in the woods. So we were empty-handed again. Twice, while we lived here, the Indians stole horses from us, and at other times they tried to, but our men drove them off. One time our men had a fight with them in the night. My present husband was with us then, and came near being killed. When we left Cheyenne we went to Sisseton agency, but only remained a few weeks. My life since then is hardly worth writing about.

My first husband died about eight years ago. Since then I have remarried to Mr. Charles Huggan. We live on a farm, near Flandrau. My only child, who was a captive with me, is the wife of Rev. John Eastman, a Presbyterian minister and a mixed-blood. They have six children, all bright, interesting and promising. When I was first married I was a Presbyterian, but Mr. Faribault and all his family were Catholics, and I became a Catholic, and am a member of that church still. I think Christian churches are like so many roads, all leading to the heavenly land. If we follow them carefully and walk uprightly in them, the All-Father will bring us to him at last.

Nancy Huggan.

Flandrau, S. D., May, 1894.

LEONAUR

ALSO FROM LEONAUR
AVAILABLE IN SOFTCOVER OR HARDCOVER WITH DUST JACKET

THE FALL OF THE MOGHUL EMPIRE OF HINDUSTAN *by H. G. Keene*—By the beginning of the nineteenth century, as British and Indian armies under Lake and Wellesley dominated the scene, a little over half a century of conflict brought the Moghul Empire to its knees.

LADY SALE'S AFGHANISTAN *by Florentia Sale*—An Indomitable Victorian Lady's Account of the Retreat from Kabul During the First Afghan War.

THE CAMPAIGN OF MAGENTA AND SOLFERINO 1859 *by Harold Carmichael Wylly*—The Decisive Conflict for the Unification of Italy.

FRENCH'S CAVALRY CAMPAIGN *by J. G. Maydon*—A Special Correspondent's View of British Army Mounted Troops During the Boer War.

CAVALRY AT WATERLOO *by Sir Evelyn Wood*—British Mounted Troops During the Campaign of 1815.

THE SUBALTERN *by George Robert Gleig*—The Experiences of an Officer of the 85th Light Infantry During the Peninsular War.

NAPOLEON AT BAY, 1814 *by F. Loraine Petre*—The Campaigns to the Fall of the First Empire.

NAPOLEON AND THE CAMPAIGN OF 1806 *by Colonel Vachée*—The Napoleonic Method of Organisation and Command to the Battles of Jena & Auerstädt.

THE COMPLETE ADVENTURES IN THE CONNAUGHT RANGERS *by William Grattan*—The 88th Regiment during the Napoleonic Wars by a Serving Officer.

BUGLER AND OFFICER OF THE RIFLES *by William Green & Harry Smith*—With the 95th (Rifles) during the Peninsular & Waterloo Campaigns of the Napoleonic Wars.

NAPOLEONIC WAR STORIES *by Sir Arthur Quiller-Couch*—Tales of soldiers, spies, battles & sieges from the Peninsular & Waterloo campaingns.

CAPTAIN OF THE 95TH (RIFLES) *by Jonathan Leach*—An officer of Wellington's sharpshooters during the Peninsular, South of France and Waterloo campaigns of the Napoleonic wars.

RIFLEMAN COSTELLO *by Edward Costello*—The adventures of a soldier of the 95th (Rifles) in the Peninsular & Waterloo Campaigns of the Napoleonic wars.

www.ingramcontent.com/pod-product-compliance
Lightning Source LLC
Chambersburg PA
CBHW031854090426
42741CB00005B/493